BOOK OF INDIAN BRAVES

BOOK OF INDIAN BRAVES

KATE DICKINSON SWEETSER

ILLUSTRATED BY GEORGE ALFRED WILLIAMS

GYAN

Published by

GYAN

Gyan Publishing House
5, Ansari Road
Daryaganj, New Delhi-110002
Phone: 011-47034999, 9811692060
E-mail: books@gyanbooks.com

Distribution Network
gyanbooks.com
India, USA, Canada, UK, Australia, France

ISBN: 978-81-212-8919-1 (PB)
First Published, 1903

2nd Impression 2023

Printed at: Gyan Press, Delhi.

BOOK OF INDIAN BRAVES

AUTHOR: KATE DICKINSON SWEETSER

CHIEF JOSEPH: PATRIOT OF THE NEZ PERCES

BOOK OF INDIAN BRAVES

BY

KATE DICKINSON SWEETSER

ILLUSTRATED BY

GEORGE ALFRED WILLIAMS

HARPER & BROTHERS PUBLISHERS
NEW YORK AND LONDON
MCMXIII

CONTENTS

ILLUSTRATIONS

POWHATAN

BOOK OF INDIAN BRAVES

POWHATAN: EMPEROR OF THIRTY TRIBES

POWHATAN, the great Werowance, or Ruler, over thirty tribes, was troubled because of disquieting reports which had been brought to him.

Not only had a settlement of pale-faced strangers been discovered scarcely two days' journey down the Chickahominy River from Weremocomoco, but half a dozen of the "pale-faces" had been seen navigating the river in a strange-looking craft, clearing away fallen trees as they went, to free the river for their progress.

Lurking in underbrush and woodland by the water's edge, more than two hundred savages watched the boat with straining eyes when it made a landing, and immediately surrounded the band of Englishmen, as the strangers proved to be.

They wore ragged clothing, such as the Indians had never before seen, and their faces and bodies were so thin and white that the stalwart red men looked at them in scorn; and when the Englishmen held out their swords and guns with gestures showing a desire to exchange them for food, the Indians grunted in derision of such weaklings and offered only a piece of bread or a handful of corn, as if to say, "This is plenty for such as you!"

But they misjudged the strength and determination of the leader of the white men, who suddenly let fly his musket, when in terror the Indians fled to the woods, leaving the pale-faces to march into the Indian village on the river-bank. There they found great piles of corn, which, however, they dared not touch for fear of an attack—and the fear was well grounded.

Suddenly with hideous cries sixty or seventy savages, their heads and shoulders brilliantly painted, and wearing only loin-cloths of skins or plaited grasses, came dancing and singing out of the woods, carrying their sacred image, or Okee, before them. They charged on the strangers, armed with clubs, shields, and bows and arrows, but were repulsed with such a shower of English bullets that their god fell over, and many of the Indians lay sprawling on the ground, while the remainder quickly disappeared again in the woods. After a hurried consultation, having decided it was unwise to make enemies of these strange men, they sent a messenger out of the forest with offers of peace and to ask for the restoration of their idol.

This was the Englishman's chance, and Captain John Smith, their leader, stepping forward, stood face to face with the dark-skinned messenger, and by dint of many gestures made himself understood.

"If you will send six unarmed men to load my boat with provisions, I will return your Okee and give you beads and copper," he said, holding out samples of these wares as he spoke, adding, "and I will also be your friend. Say this to your comrades while we await their answer."

They had not long to wait. The messenger disappeared in the woods and presently came back surrounded by a whooping, dancing crowd of Indians, carrying wild fowl and bread, in exchange for which the Englishmen gave the trinkets they had promised, and so delighted were the child-like savages that when the white men took leave of them they were all singing and dancing in uproarious token of friendship for the departing ones, although probably relieved to have them go.

All this was told to Powhatan, who was then at his favorite dwelling-place, Weremocomoco, on the York River. In silence he received the communication, and gave no visible sign of the alarm it aroused in him, yet his heart was heavy with forebodings. Why had these strangers come to the haunts of the red men? Would they be friends or foes to the Indian?

These questions were scornfully set aside, for was not he, Powhatan, the powerful Werowance over all the tribes of Powhatans, to whom all paid tribute of "skinnes, beads, copper, pearls, deere, turkies, wild beasts, and corne"? Were not his commands such as no one in his dominion dared disobey? Did not all his people give him both obedience and adoration? Further than that, had he not a fleet of which to be proud, including, as it did, a collection of dugouts, large and small, which was second to none belonging to alien tribes?

And, too, his body-guard was one such as would strike awe and fear to the heart of any invading foe, for every night at the four corners of his dwelling four sentinels were stationed, and at every half-hour one of the guard would make a low call by shaking his lips, with his fingers between them, whereupon every other sentinel would answer in turn; and if any failed to reply, then an officer would go forth and beat the delinquent severely.

More than this, if these strangers should attempt to attack his person, he had a half-dozen residences to which he could flee.

Weremocomoco could be abandoned for Orapakes, and that in turn for Powhatan, and by flight and by war surely he could maintain the dignity and rights of the Indians, so long as he had a warrior left to help him wage war or keep peace. But let the white man once seriously encroach on Indian territory, and there would be trouble wide-spread and devastating for him and all his pale-faced comrades!

So mused Powhatan, even while receiving the disconcerting news from a breathless young warrior; then, rising and drawing his great skin mantle around him with proud dignity, he waved his informers back, and, stalking away through the woods with such dignified bearing as befitted the leader of his people, hastily called together his oldest and wisest chiefs to discuss means of protection against a possible danger. Far into the night the heart of the forest glowed with the red flare of the council-fire, and shadowy forms gathered around it, talking long and solemnly about the white men's intentions. When at last the braves took their silent way back to wigwam and mat-house, it had been decided to strengthen Powhatan's body-guard from between forty and fifty of the tallest men in his dominions to several hundred; to keep a number of fleet-footed young braves in daily touch with the settlement of strangers down the river, and to instruct all the young men of the tribes that whenever a white man was seen near an Indian settlement there was to be instant alarm and pursuit. Then let the pale-faces do what they would—Powhatan and his warriors were ready for them!

Meanwhile the little band of English colonists, near the mouth of the river James, were busy erecting such cabins as were suitable to live in, and making all sorts of rude articles of furniture which were necessary for use in their rough forest life. Among the ruling spirits of the colony were Captain Newport, Captain Bartholomew Gosnold, and Captain John Smith, the latter a soldier of fortune who had voyaged around the world, been in captivity among the Turks, and experienced all sorts of thrilling adventures before undertaking the trip to the new-found world of America, and he it was whose enthusiasm and resources kept the colonists from sinking into the mire of despondency in those early days when provisions ran low, the location of the settlement proved so unhealthy that daily new graves were dug, and all nature seemed conspiring to make the attempt to colonize Virginia a complete failure. Although by reason of his blunt way of speaking and of his peremptory manner in setting every one to work Captain Smith was not popular among the settlers, yet all looked to him to take the initiative in matters pertaining to the welfare of the colony, and, provisions being scarce, he went on a voyage of discovery up the Chickahominy River, as we have seen, returning with a boat-load of provisions. Instead of applauding him for this, the idle and unruly—of whom there were a large number in the colony—blamed him for not having followed the river to its source and found a possible store of gold or a passage to the South Sea, which they were constantly expecting to discover.

Captain Smith bore their reproaches and taunts for only a short time, then in midwinter he set off again, taking with him a sufficient crew to manage a barge, also a lighter boat which could navigate the narrower streams of the upper Chickahominy. As before, he cut away trees to clear a passage for the smaller boat, and in it worked his way twenty miles up the river, where he was rewarded by discovering in the "slashes," as swampy meadows are called in Virginia, not gold or a passage to the South Sea, but the headwaters of the river for which he was looking.

During his absence the men he had left in charge of the barge were killed by a band of savages, who later captured the brave captain himself, and led him in a triumphal procession from town to town, to be stared at with curious eyes by savages who had never before seen a white man.

Marching Indian file, the long line of fierce warriors, with their heads and shoulders gaily painted, wound its way through meadow, field, and forest, Opechancanough, a brother of Powhatan, marching in the center, with the English firearms carried before him as trophies. Captain Smith followed, led by three stalwart Indians, who gripped him by the arm, while six other men marched on either side in file as flank guards to prevent his escape.

In this way the long line of braves tramped on to the forest settlement of Orapakes, then farther, to the residence of Opechancanough at Pamunkey, winding its slow way to the dwelling of Opitchipan, another brother of Powhatan, and more than once during the march Captain Smith's life was in danger. At last a piece of startling news was passed from Indian to Indian, and finally interpreted to the prisoner.

Powhatan, the great Werowance over thirty tribes, had sent his command. He wished to see this white leader who had been taken captive.

At once the procession of warriors turned toward Weremocomoco, and when they came in sight of the settlement they were surrounded by a crowd of eager savages who had gathered to catch a glimpse of the pale-faced prisoner. After a long halt came the summons to Powhatan's presence, and a few moments later the wary old Werowance received the white-faced captain.

With majestic dignity and inscrutable reserve, Powhatan bowed a welcome, looking every inch a ruler as he reclined on a seat something like a bedstead, with a great robe of racoon-skins thrown over his stalwart figure. On either side of him sat a young woman, and ranged along each wall of the building were two rows of other women in the rear, and two rows of men in the front. All had their heads and shoulders painted red, while some of the women wore the white down of birds on their garments and some had long chains of white beads about their necks.

As the prisoner stood before Powhatan there was a mighty shout, and immediately the Queen of Appamattock, an Indian woman, with an elaborately decorated person and garment, brought water to wash his hands, while another followed with a bunch of feathers to serve the purpose of a towel.

Then followed an elaborate feast and a long debate among Powhatan's councilors, while Captain Smith waited to know his fate.

The debate was over. Powhatan had given his commands. Solemnly two Indians rolled two large stones before the great Ruler, and, laying rough hands on Captain Smith, dragged him to Powhatan's feet, forcing his head down on the stones. Brave as he was, the Captain trembled. The clubs of the stalwart Indians were raised, ready to beat out his brains.

There was the sound of rushing feet, a slight girlish figure shot through the watching crowd, fell on her knees before Powhatan, and pleaded for the Captain's life. It was Pocahontas, Powhatan's "dearest daughter," a girl of twelve, who, with her first look at Smith's white face and expressive eyes, had thrilled with interest in this man of a different race from her own, who, she instinctively felt, was high above her people in intelligence. Should an Indian kill him as they kill beasts of prey? Never! She clung to

Powhatan's robe with words of entreaty, but Powhatan did not notice her. Again the clubs were raised. With a shriek Pocahontas ran to Smith's side, clasped his head in her arms, and laid her own dark head above his. To kill him would be to kill his child, and Powhatan surrendered. Holding up a restraining hand to the men with uplifted clubs, he uttered a solemn decree. The prisoner should live to make hatchets for him and belts for his daughter, he announced—an evident compromise with his dignity as a ruler and his keen interest in this man of an alien race.

One quick glance passed between Captain Smith and Pocahontas, and the young girl's eyes grew starry with exultation as she ran back among the throng, filled with a determination to be forever the loyal friend of the white men; and loyally did she keep that vow.

Although Powhatan had twenty sons and eleven daughters, none of them had the place in his affection held by this "dearest daughter," Pocahontas, whose real name, *Matoake*, was concealed from the English because of an Indian superstition that if they knew her real name they might do her harm. So she became known as Pocahontas, or "playful," and at the time she rescued the Captain she was a slight slip of a girl, whose dusky face showed a finely chiseled nose, eyes full of charm, whether sparkling with joy or melting with tenderness, and hair black as a crow's wing, with never a curl in it, adorned with a drooping white plume, in sign of being the daughter of a great ruler. She wore a robe of soft doeskin girdled at the waist; glistening on her shapely feet were beaded moccasins; and there was a glint of coral bracelets on her slim arms. Altogether, from hair to toe the maiden radiated a charm none could gainsay, and to the man whose life she saved she looked no less than beautiful.

POCAHONTAS SAVES CAPTAIN JOHN SMITH

POWHATAN

For two days after pardoning him, Powhatan kept the Captain a prisoner, then he was led to a council-house in the dense woods and seated on a mat before the fire, when suddenly Powhatan appeared before him, dressed fantastically, and followed by two hundred warriors as much begrimed, painted, and decorated as himself. They all rushed in and surrounded Smith, who by this time expected danger at any moment, and told him that they were his friends, and that he was to return to Jamestown for the purpose of sending back to Powhatan two great guns and a grindstone, for which favors Powhatan would give him the country of Capahowsick, and forever honor him as his own son.

This was good news to the Captain, whose only desire was to return to the colony, and at once he was allowed to set out for Jamestown, with an escort of twelve Indians, who were to carry back the weapons and grindstone to Powhatan.

Arriving at the English colony, clever Captain Smith at once showed the Indians two long cannon purposely loaded with stones, which were discharged among the icicle-laden branches of the trees to terrify the savages. They were then told to lift the grindstone, which they could scarcely move, and when Captain Smith offered to send back beads and copper instead of the desired articles the offer was thankfully accepted. The guides went happily off with their trinkets, and for several months afterward only friendly Indians were seen at the settlement.

Then Captain Smith, and Captain Newport, who had just arrived from a visit to England and was very anxious to see the famous Indian ruler, made a trip together to Weremocomoco. Powhatan received them in state, lying on his bed of mats, clad in a magnificent fur mantle, with his brilliantly embroidered pillow of skins lying beside him, and, as usual, he was flanked by his body-guard of stalwart armed young Indians and by many other men and women, who sang and danced in the Englishmen's honor.

Captain Newport then suggested that he had brought articles with him to barter for corn, and urged Powhatan to trade with him, but the great Werowance replied loftily:

"Captain Newport, it is not agreeable to my greatness to truck in this peddling manner for trifles. I am a great Werowance, and I esteem you the same. Therefore, lay me down all your commodities, what I like I will take, and in return you shall have what I conceive to be a fair value."

Captain Smith shook his head, to warn Newport of the risk he would incur if he accepted the offer, but Newport refused to take advice, and his wares were spread out for Powhatan's inspection. With an air of indifference the chief inspected each article, selected such as he liked best, then valued his own corn at such a high price that Newport only received four bushels where he had counted on twenty hogsheads—and Powhatan had proved his shrewdness at bargaining!

Nettled at his companion's lack of diplomacy, Captain Smith now tried his hand at trading. Taking up some blue beads, he so held them that they glittered in the strong light and at once attracted Powhatan's attention.

"What will you take for them?" he asked.

Smith shook his head. "I cannot part with them," he said, "being composed of a rare substance of the color of the sky and only fit to be worn by the greatest kings of the world; they are too valuable to be bartered in ordinary trade."

Powhatan's eyes gleamed. Jewels fit for a king were the ornaments for Powhatan. He offered more corn, but Smith only shook his head. More and more eager grew Powhatan, and finally offered between two and three hundred bushels of corn for a pound or two of the beads. With apparent reluctance Smith closed the bargain, Newport gazing at him in wide-eyed admiration.

Opechancanough then arrived, and a similar bargain was made with him. Blue beads soon became so valuable that none but the great Werowances and their wives dared wear them, for they were considered to be symbols of royalty, and by them Captain Smith had obtained his supply of corn.

But it was not alone on beads that Powhatan fixed longing eyes. Daily his desire for English weapons and tools grew deeper, and he determined to obtain them at any price. As a result of deep deliberation he sent Newport, who was returning to England, a present of twenty fine turkeys, requesting in return as many swords; and gleeful he was when his messengers brought back the coveted arms from the good-natured Captain. At once he despatched another messenger to Captain Smith, with a similar gift and request, but this time the messenger returned empty-handed!

Powhatan was angry, and, calling together his councilors and the younger warriors of the tribe, he gave orders to take firearms from the colonists wherever and in whatever manner they could be taken, saying that the Indians must have a supply of them at once for their own safety.

A few days later Smith caught a party of marauding Indians outside the Jamestown fort, skulking away with swords they had stolen, and had them promptly whipped and imprisoned. Powhatan, thus checkmated, became the victim of fierce jealousy, and a jealous Indian is the most vindictive creature in the world.

He brooded long on how to gain his end, and decided

that through Pocahontas he could best accomplish it; so, calling her to him, he bade her go to Jamestown, taking messengers with corn and wild fowl, and to beg Captain Smith's pardon for the injury done by "some of his disorderly warriors," also to ask that those Indians be freed this time on their good behavior.

With downcast eyes and demure docility the maiden accepted the charge, and little did her father dream that a trip to the English settlement was no novelty to her, for since the day when she saved Smith's life she had made many secret visits to the colonists, carrying them needed provisions and winning the admiration and respect of the Englishmen by her gracious loyalty.

Captain Smith received both guest and gifts with courteous thanks, and after a brief talk with Pocahontas, in the presence of all the colonists, he liberated the captured Indians, "only for the sake of Pocahontas," so he said, and friendly relations between the Indians and white men were again resumed for a time.

Then Captain Newport came back again from England, bringing with him presents with which he hoped to make Powhatan a more loyal ally of the English. Among the gifts were a splendid basin and pitcher, a bedstead, bed linen, and a real crown, sent by King James himself, under the absurd idea that by its glitter and by the pomp of a coronation ceremony the old chief could be more easily made a royal subject.

Powhatan must be invited to Jamestown to receive his gifts. There was also need of a boat-load of corn. As usual, Captain Smith volunteered his services for the expedition to Weremocomoco, and departed, taking with him four companions. To their disappointment, Powhatan was absent, visiting a neighboring tribe, but pretty Pocahontas greeted them with eager cordiality, and at once despatched messengers for her father, while she and her attendants entertained their guests in a remarkable way.

Having been seated in an open field near the edge of the woods, they heard a hideous noise, and quickly seized their weapons, fearing an attack. Instead, Pocahontas, flitting like a fawn, ran out of the woods with small deer antlers on her head and a robe of otter-skin around her shoulders, while another fell from her waist down to her beaded moccasins. At her back hung a quiver of arrows, and she carried a small cedar bow on her arm.

Flourishing this around her head, she flitted back, still laughing, to the woods and soon appeared again, leading a party of girls singing and dancing, their bodies painted with many colors, wearing girdles of green leaves from the waist down, all horned like Pocahontas and brandishing swords and pot-sticks.

For an hour they danced in a ring around the fire, laughing and singing and crying out; then they danced away, and presently came back without their strange costumes, to spread a lavish supper for the colonists, after which they all escorted the Englishmen back to their wigwams, lighting their path with torches and crying out a merry farewell when they parted from their guests for the night.

Powhatan arrived on the next day with his impressive body-guard, and Smith gave the invitation to visit Jamestown, not only to receive his gifts, but to talk over the project of conducting a campaign with the English against the Monacans, a nation with whom Powhatan was at war; also to discuss an expedition to discover the South Sea, which the English had been led to believe was but a short distance back from Weremocomoco.

There was a long silence. Not a trace of expression was

on Powhatan's inscrutable face. Rising, he threw an end of his robe over his shoulder with the air of a haughty monarch.

"If your King has sent me presents," he said, "I also am a King. Here I will stay eight days to receive them. Your father [meaning Newport] is to come to me, not I to him, nor yet to your fort. . . . As for the Monacans, I can avenge my own injuries. As for any salt-water beyond the mountains, the relations you have had are false."

Taking up a stick, he began to draw a map of the country, as he knew it, on the ground, but he would converse no further, and Captain Smith was obliged to return to Jamestown with the old Werowance's refusal to visit the colonists.

Not wishing to offend his Majesty King James, Newport felt it necessary in some way to present the crown and carry out the coronation ceremony; so he and Captain Smith, taking with them the gifts, went back to Weremocomoco. Powhatan received them graciously, and they presented him with the bedstead and basin and pitcher, in which novelties he showed a keen delight. Then Captain Smith tried to make him put on the coronation robes, but with haughty dignity he drew away, wrapped his own mantle about him, and refused to exchange it for the new splendor.

Namontack, his trusty Indian boy, who at Powhatan's desire had accompanied Captain Newport to England and back, hastily assured the old monarch that the garments were such as were worn by the English and would do him no harm. Standing as stiff and straight as a wooden image, Powhatan then submitted to be dressed in the robe of royalty and was told to kneel while the crown was placed on his head. With frightened eyes and imperturbable resolve he stood more stiff and straight than before, watching the Englishmen bend and bow and kneel in example of what he ought to do—but still rigidly erect.

Time was going—the coronation must take place; in despair Captain Smith laid a powerful hand on the Werowance's broad shoulders until he stooped a little. The crown was hastily placed on his head, and a volley of shots was fired as a signal that the ceremony was accomplished. Powhatan, indignant, frightened, and sure now that he had been trapped, sprang free like a wild creature, and it took the combined efforts of the two captains to soothe him and to make him understand that the shots were a part of the programme.

Having at last been calmed, the new-made Emperor received further explanations with gracious condescension, and, beckoning to Namontack, bade him give his discarded moccasins and mantle to Captain Newport, as if to imply that even the cast-off garments of an emperor were a gift of value.

With rueful amusement the Captain accepted his gift, but explained that, more than moccasins or mantles, he wished Powhatan's help in attacking the Monacans. Powhatan's refusal was firm. None of his men except the trusty Namontack, who he knew would not betray him, should go on the expedition, he said. The refusal was made civilly, however, and accompanied by a present of several bushels of corn, so it was not possible to show any resentment at the firmness of the new-made Emperor; and neither then nor in the following months were there any open hostilities between the Indians and the Jamestown settlers, but in Powhatan's heart bitter jealousy had been growing. He felt hatred for these men with their coveted weapons and their broader intelligence, and gave command that no Indians were to trade with the English. This angered Captain Smith so deeply that he had a great desire to surprise Powhatan and carry away by force his stores of provisions, but neither he nor the Emperor made a move to show his feelings.

Then, to Smith's surprise, there came to Jamestown messengers from Powhatan, inviting the Captain to visit Weremocomoco again, and suggesting that he bring a grindstone, some muskets, a cock and hen, beads and copper, for which he would be paid by a ship-load of corn.

Always ready for adventures, Captain Smith promptly accepted the invitation, and with forty volunteers set off on his journey, spending the first night at Warrasqueak, where a friendly old chief cautioned him not to go farther, as Powhatan had sent for the white men this time only to cut their throats.

The prospect was not a cheerful one, and the Captain had to inspire his comrades with ringing words of courage before they would accompany him farther, but at last all agreed to go, and they went on to Kekoughtan, where such a heavy storm came up that they were obliged to remain there among the Indians over Christmas. So royally were they treated that, as they afterward told, they had "never been more merry in their lives, lodged by better fires or fed with greater plenty of good bread, fish, flesh, and wild fowl."

Meanwhile, it was evident to all his councilors that Powhatan was deciding some important question. By the council-fire or in warfare he maintained such a brooding silence that all knew his thoughts were occupied with matters of grave importance. Then Captain Smith and his companions arrived, landed, and were housed in a deserted wigwam in the woods, and asked for provisions. Powhatan bade Namontack take them enough food for two days, but on the third day sent this message to the Captain:

"When are you going away? Your visit was not anticipated, and we Powhatans have too limited a supply of corn to supply you much longer, although if you will give us forty swords perhaps forty baskets would be collected."

Concealing his anger, Smith retorted:

"Ask the Emperor if he has forgotten his invitation to us to visit him?"

The message was carried to Powhatan by the very men he had sent to Jamestown with his invitation, and, being confronted by them, he was obliged to remember what he wished to forget, and tried to make a joke of his rudeness.

Without further delay Smith proposed to trade, but Powhatan refused to take anything but guns and swords, and at such a high price that finally the Captain showed his displeasure, saying he had complied with all the Emperor's requests, and did not deserve such treatment. To this Powhatan answered gravely:

"We have but little corn, but what we can spare shall be brought two days hence. As to your coming here, I have some doubt about the reason for it. I am told by my men that you came not to trade, but to invade my people and to possess my country. This makes me less ready to believe you, and frightens my people from bringing in my corn. Therefore, to relieve that fear, leave your arms aboard your boats, since they are needless here where we are all friends and forever Powhatans."

Doubtless the information to which the Emperor alluded had been given him by several Germans who had deserted the colonists to live with the Indians, and Smith was quick-witted enough to know that a critical moment in the intercourse between the Powhatans and his men had come. Cleverly he retorted to the Emperor, who in turn answered him back, and the whole day was spent in exchanging messages. Only one trade was made, when Smith wrangled Powhatan out of eighty bushels of corn in exchange for a copper kettle, on which, seeing Powhatan's liking for it, he set an absurdly high price, saying that because of the scarcity of corn he would accept that quantity at present, provided he should have as much the next year, or the Manakin country if the conditions were not complied with—which proposal was sharp enough to set even a savage on his guard. With solemn, keen eyes Powhatan looked at the Captain; then he said:

"I am now grown old and must soon die, and the succession must descend in order to my brothers, and then to my two sisters and their two daughters. . . . I wish that your love to us might not be less than ours to you. Why should you take by force that from us which you can have by love? Why should you destroy us who have provided you with food? What can you get by war? We can hide our provisions and fly into our woods, and then you must famish by wronging your friends. What is the cause of your jealousy? You see us unarmed and willing to supply your wants if you will come in a friendly manner, and not with swords and guns as to invade an enemy. I am not so simple as not to know it is better to eat good meat, sleep quietly, to laugh and be merry with the English, and, being their friend, to have copper hatchets and whatever else I want, than to fly from all, to lie cold in the woods, feed upon acorns, roots, and such trash, and to be so hunted that I cannot rest, eat, or sleep. In such circumstances my men must watch, and if a twig should but break all would cry out, 'Here comes Captain Smith,' and so in this miserable manner to end my miserable life, and this might soon be your fate, too, through your rashness and unadvisedness. I therefore exhort you to peaceable councils, and above all I insist that the guns and swords, the cause of all our jealousy and uneasiness, be sent away."

Captain Smith retorted that the colonists meant the Indians no harm, that had they desired to injure them it could easily have been achieved, adding, "Your people coming to Jamestown are entertained with their bows and arrows without any exceptions, we esteeming it with you, as it is with us, to wear our arms as our apparel. As for the danger of our enemies, in such wars lies our chiefest pleasure; for your riches we have no use; as for hiding your provision, or by your flying to the woods, we shall not so unadvisedly starve as you conclude; your friendly care in that behalf is needless, for we have a rule to find beyond your knowledge."

Certainly the glib Captain and the inscrutable Emperor were well matched in repartee, and neither one was to be caught off his guard. Trading was again begun, and again Powhatan showed dissatisfaction that he could not have his way.

"Captain Smith," he said, "I never used any Werowance as kindly as yourself, yet from you I receive the least kindness of any. Captain Newport gave me swords, copper, clothes, or whatever I desired, . . . and would send away his guns when requested. No one refuses to lie at my feet or do what I demand but only you. Of you I can have nothing but what you value not, and yet you will have whatever you please. Captain Newport you called father, and so you call me, but I see, in spite of us both, you will do what you will and we must both study to humor and content you. But if you intend so friendly as you say, send away your arms, for you see my undesigning simplicity and friendship cause me thus nakedly to forget myself."

Powhatan was right. Captain Smith was determined to

have his way, and he saw that nothing was to be gained by this battle of words. It was evident to him that Powhatan while he talked was only watching with sharp eyes for a chance to get the Englishmen in his power. Something decisive must be done. Turning to a group of Indians who were friendly, the Captain asked them to go to the river and break the ice so that his boat might land and his men take away the corn he had bought of Powhatan. His plan was to capture the old Emperor as soon as the men arrived, but to keep Powhatan from suspecting this he again spoke to him.

"Powhatan," he said, "you must know as I have but one God, I honor but one King, and I live not here as your subject but as your friend, to pleasure you with what I can. By the gifts you bestow on me you gain more than by trade, yet, would you visit me as I visit you, you should know it is not our custom to sell our courtesies as a vendable commodity. Bring all your country with you for your guard, I will not dislike you as being over-jealous. But to content you, to-morrow I will leave my arms and trust your promise. I call you father indeed, and as a father you shall see I will love you, but the small care you have for such a child caused my men to persuade me to look to myself."

Powhatan was not fooled by this. Well he knew that the Captain was playing the same game of strategy as he was, and he feared that the white man would be more successful at it than he had been. Slyly beckoning a young warrior, he gave a whispered command, and two squaws in gaily decorated robes ran forward and squatting at Smith's feet, engaged his attention by singing and by the telling of tribal tales. Stealthily, silently, Powhatan rose, stole quietly away, and fled to a safe retreat, taking with him provisions as well as women and children.

Immediately the Powhatan warriors surrounded the Englishmen, who fought back the throng of Indians with swords, Indian shields, and pistols; and the savages fell over one another in fear, fleeing in every direction, while the Captain and his comrades went back to their woodland quarters in safety, to await high tide, when they would be able to float away.

The news of his warriors' defeat was carried to Powhatan's hiding-place, and he at once sent one of his most convincing orators with a handsome bracelet as a present to the Captain, and the explanation that he, Powhatan, had only fled because he was afraid of the English arms, and again begged that they might be laid aside, when he would return, bringing with him an abundance of corn for the colonists. To this Smith sent back a firm refusal, and Powhatan, enraged, called to his retreat all the warriors he could gather, and ordered them to surprise and kill the Englishmen on the next night. So intent on giving this command was he that he did not notice the slight figure of Pocahontas crouching at the edge of the forest as he spoke.

That evening, after the fall of twilight, Captain Smith, seated alone in his forest wigwam, heard the swift approach of feet, and the Indian maiden stood beside him, her eyes big with terror and with appeal.

"Captain Smith," she said, "great cheer will be sent you by and by, but Powhatan and all the power he can make will after come and kill you all, if they that bring you the cheer do not kill you with your own weapons when you are at supper. Therefore if you would live I wish you presently to be gone."

It was a brave act of Pocahontas to come there to him through the forest, and the Captain was touched. He expressed his thanks in hearty words, offering her as a token of his appreciation the rarest trinkets he possessed, but Pocahontas shook her head, with tears in her starry eyes.

"I dare not," she said, "to be seen to have any, for if Powhatan should know it I am but dead." With that she ran away like a deer into the woods and disappeared.

Presently eight or ten stalwart Indians came bearing great platters of food. They begged the Captain to put out the matches to their guns, for the smoke "made them sick," they said, and they wished him to sit down to eat; but the Captain shook his head and motioned to the Indians to taste each dish first, then sent them back to Powhatan, asking him to make haste and return, as he was awaiting him.

To this there was no answer, but soon other messengers bearing unimportant messages arrived, evidently sent to keep a watch on the doings of the English, and the night passed, with no open hostilities, but with messengers coming and going. Then at high tide, unmolested, the Captain and his companions were able to depart.

While Captain Smith had been away from Jamestown a boat-load of the colonists had been drowned in a terrible storm, and a settler, Mr. Wyffin, set out for Weremocomoco to carry the tidings to Captain Smith. On arriving there he found that the Englishmen had left, and saw preparations for war on every side. Being one of the colonists, his life would have been in danger, but Pocahontas hid him until it was safe to send him away, and when the Indians started in pursuit she directed them wrongly, and so once again the loyal maiden saved a white man's life.

For some time after Captain Smith's party returned to Jamestown there was a truce between the Indians and the settlers, yet Powhatan's hatred of the aliens, who possessed such weapons and such intelligence, was smoldering, and in one way or another he secured a large number of the coveted firearms. Then he captured and held as prisoners several Englishmen, for which act the colonists were determined to have revenge.

At that time Pocahontas was visiting among the Potomacs, a neighboring tribe, on the river of that name, probably sent there by her father, who distrusted her intimacy with the white men and wished to have her farther away from them. Captain Argall, an Englishman, went to trade with the Potomacs, and, hearing that Pocahontas was there among their tribe, a brilliant scheme for revenge on Powhatan occurred to him. He would capture the Emperor's "dearest daughter" and hold her for a ransom.

To gain his end he bribed an old Indian named Japazaws, with his wife, to betray Pocahontas into his power, offering the irresistible bribe of a copper kettle in exchange for the deed. In the presence of Pocahontas the old woman begged to be allowed to visit the English ship at anchor off shore, but Japazaws sternly refused the request, saying she could not go unless accompanied by some other woman, and at last threatened to beat her if she begged any longer. Pocahontas's tender heart being touched at this, she offered to go with the woman, and at once the party were taken on board the ship and entertained so lavishly that the two delighted old schemers kept treading on Captain Argall's toes during supper to show their joy.

Supper over, Pocahontas was detained in the gun-room while the boat got under way; then the captain, sending for her, told her that she was to remain with him. Pocahontas shrieked and sank back in terror, but, on hearing the reason of her capture, recovered her spirits and entered into the plan with enthusiastic interest, realizing that no harm was to be done her, and hoping to bring about peace between her people and the English.

Captain Argall immediately sent a messenger to Powhatan, saying that his daughter was a prisoner of the English, but that if he would send home the men whom he had captured, with such weapons and tools as had been stolen from the colonists, and a quantity of corn, his "delight and darling" should be restored to him.

There was a great excitement among the Powhatans when this news was received, but Powhatan himself preserved an inscrutable reserve. With grim calmness he sent back word to the Englishmen by the messenger that they were to take good care of Pocahontas and that he would accede to the conditions of her rescue.

But one month, two, and a third went by, with no word from him, as his desire for English weapons and his affection for his daughter were at war in his heart. At the end of the third month, however, he sent to Jamestown seven of the captive colonists, with a message that he would also send a large amount of corn and be forever their friend if they would give up his daughter.

Captain Smith sent back this answer:

"Your daughter shall be well used, but we cannot believe the rest of our arms are either lost or stolen from you, and, therefore, till you send them back we will keep your daughter."

Powhatan made no answer to this, and for so long a time was silent that the Englishmen grew impatient with him. Although since the coming of Pocahontas to Jamestown all the colonists had become deeply attached to the vivacious young girl and would miss her sadly when she left their little settlement, yet at the end of a year they were so irritated at Powhatan's silence that Sir Thomas Dale, taking with him Pocahontas and one hundred and fifty men, embarked for Weremocomoco.

Powhatan was not there. He was still in hiding, and when the English told the Indians who received them that they had come to give up Pocahontas and to receive the promised return of arms and men, the warriors received both overtures and threats with scorn and open hostility, and there were several skirmishes in which much Indian property was destroyed.

Peace was finally made, and two of Pocahontas's brothers were interviewed and allowed to go on board the boat to visit their sister. Their joy at seeing her rosy and well deepened into awe, when with downcast eyes and flushed cheeks she told them of her attachment to Mr. John Rolfe, one of the finest gentlemen in the English colony, who, months before, had begun to convert the little pagan to the Christian religion, and had ended by falling in love with her, which love she returned. This savored of the miraculous to her stalwart, bronze-skinned brothers of a savage race, and, hastening from the boat, they went at once to their father's retreat, to tell him the great piece of news. For once in his life an expression of fierce exultation gleamed in the black eyes of the Emperor. His daughter, the child of an Indian Werowance, the wife of an Englishman? The two races to be united? Surely this would be a greater advantage to his tribe than all the firearms which could be bought or stolen!

Within ten days an old uncle of Pocahontas's, together with her two brothers, arrived at Jamestown to witness the ceremony, carrying her father's sanction to her marriage, but no amount of urging could prevail on the old chief himself to be present, as he had a great fear of visiting the home of the colonists.

Then in the presence of a large number of her devoted English friends and three of her own tribe and kin, Pocahontas was first baptized in Christian baptism; and on an April day in 1614 a strange bridal procession moved up the aisle of the little Jamestown church: the bridegroom, a bright-eyed, earnest young Englishman; the girlish bride, a dusky Indian; her attendants, two bronzed young braves. At the altar a minister of the colony repeated the simple service, and Pocahontas in her pretty but imperfect English repeated her marriage vows, then put on the wedding-ring of civilized races, as calmly as though she had never been a wild bird of the forest.

Powhatan, who still remained in retreat at Matchcat, several miles beyond Weremocomoco, spent his daughter's wedding-day in such deep absorption that even his oldest warrior dared not approach him in ordinary conversation; but it was noticed that he held his head higher and spoke with more majestic dignity than before, and from that day he never again gave an order to do an injury to, or to violate the peace with, one of that race to which his daughter's marriage had allied him.

With such advantages resulting from the marriage of Pocahontas to one of their number, Ralph Hamer, another colonist, was sent by Sir Thomas Dale, some months later, to secure for Sir Thomas himself another daughter of the Indian Emperor.

Powhatan was found by Hamer in his forest retreat, and received his guest civilly. When evening came, with Powhatan he was seated before the fire in the Emperor's great wigwam, while Englishman and chief smoked the pipe of peace together. Powhatan then inquired for his daughter's health and happiness, and Hamer replied that she was so content she would on no account return to live with Powhatan. A grim smile overspread the old chief's face, and with no remark on the subject he abruptly asked Hamer why he had visited him. Hamer then drew out and presented several gifts sent by Sir Thomas Dale, and added, "Sir Thomas desires your youngest daughter in marriage, and begs that she may return with me to make her sister a visit in order to become acquainted with the life at Jamestown.

Powhatan, looking every inch a king, in his great fur robe and elaborate head-dress, listened gravely to this proposal from an Englishman for the hand of his second child.

Satisfaction could go no further, but of this he gave no sign; and when Mr. Hamer had finished speaking the chief thanked him for the honor he had conferred by his proposal, but said gravely he regretted having only a few days before sold his daughter to a great Werowance living three days' journey away, for three bushels of Roanoke.

Hamer with equal gravity suggested that a ruler of his greatness could recall his permission if he so chose, especially as his daughter was only twelve years old; that in such a case Sir Thomas Dale would give in exchange for her three times the value of the Roanoke in hatchets and copper.

Solemnly the Emperor bowed in recognition of the courtesy, and with equal solemnity set aside the offer. He could not live without seeing his daughter every day, he said, which would be impossible if she went among the colonists, as he had resolved never to put himself in their power by visiting them, despite his friendship with them; that he had already given up one child to them; that if she should die he would give up the other in token of friendship. With pathetic dignity he added:

"I hold it not a brotherly part for your King to endeavor

to bereave me of my two darling children at once. Give him to understand that if he had no pledge at all, he need not distrust any injury from me or my people. There has already been too much of blood and war; too many of my people and of his have already fallen in our strife, and by my occasion there shall never be any more, . . . for I am grown old and would gladly end my remaining days in peace and quiet. Even if the English should offer me injury, I should not resent it. My country is large enough, and I would remove myself farther from you. I hope this will give satisfaction to my brother. He cannot have my daughter. If he is not satisfied, I will move three days' journey from him and never see Englishmen more."

He relapsed into an unyielding silence. The pipe of peace had long since been extinguished; the great forest logs were smoldering in a last red flare, and the big wigwam was in semi-darkness, showing the shadowy form of the mighty Werowance sitting before the dying fire in a dim outline of dignity and repose.

Back to the days of his supremacy as a young warrior; back to the joy of his mighty conquests, to the days of Pocahontas's childhood; forward to the days when, as Lady Rebecca, the wife of a man in whose veins ran the blood of an alien people, she should be the pride both of his race and of the English, roved the memories and thoughts of the old Indian Emperor, forgetful now of the guest beside him. Bending over him for a moment, to study the strong, inscrutable face of the great chief, Hamer tiptoed softly away, leaving Powhatan, the mighty Werowance over thirty tribes, the far-famed Indian Emperor, alone—to muse, to dream, and to hope.

OSCEOLA

OSCEOLA: WAR-CHIEF OF THE SEMINOLES

FORT KING lay scorching in the rays of the midday sun. Under the protecting shadow of the stockade General Thompson and his troopers were ranged in military order, waiting, with the treaty of Payne's Landing on a table before them—a treaty which the Seminoles declared they had been tricked into signing.

Beside this treaty lay its sister document, which the savages had also signed in ignorance that by so doing they declared themselves content to move from their beloved Florida to lands beyond the Mississippi, which they did not wish to occupy, allotted them by an unfriendly government.

Under the lee of the stockade the soldiers waited. Through the depths of the great swamp near by wound a long trail of Indian braves, gaudy with paint and plumes, marching to the fort in the forest shade of live-oaks and cypresses deep-garlanded with Southern moss. Rounding the stockade, the red men lined up, facing the troopers, and with nods and grunts of greeting declared themselves ready for the conference to which they had been called.

Micanopy, veteran chief of the Seminoles, headed the line, and beside him stood the brilliant young warrior As-se-he-ho-lar, called Osceola, or "Black Drink," who was soon to become war-chief of his tribe by reason of his daring and ability. Beyond him stood Tiger Tail, Jumper, Alligator, and many other braves, all willing to hear what the white men had to say for themselves, but firm in their determination to resist the decree that would push their tribe out of Florida into a country for which they had no liking.

General Thompson acknowledged the Indians' greeting; then, stepping forward, spoke slowly, weighing his words:

"The Great Father at Washington, Andrew Jackson," he said, "has now decided to enforce the treaty of Payne's Landing, signed by your chiefs."

Micanopy groaned, a younger chief threw up his arms in a wild, threatening gesture, and there was a chorus of menacing sounds from the line of braves. Osceola alone remained silent and impassive while he heard what the general had to say. Then, leaning over, he whispered to Micanopy, telling the old warrior what to reply to the general, as he himself was not allowed to speak, not being a chief.

Micanopy shook his head at the young warrior's whisper, as if to show that he did not approve of the ideas of one who was flushed by the vigor of youth and health and wished to go to the extreme of daring; but he said nothing until after three sub-chiefs who had been called on to speak had all denied that the treaty had been signed by the Seminoles. The last chief added:

"We signed a treaty in 1821 that was supposed to hold good for twenty years, and why should we have signed another until the time limit of that had expired?"

Then old Micanopy, in answer to Osceola's meaning glance, rose and said, firmly, "I did *not* sign the treaty of Payne's Landing. I only extended my hand to do so." With eyes fixed on the general's face, he added, "The treaty was to *examine* the country—not to occupy it."

Jumper muttered, "The treaty was made to keep the white men quiet and to obtain provisions!" Another and another of the braves added their testimony, which agreed with what had been already said. The entire assemblage

OSCEOLA: WAR-CHIEF OF THE SEMINOLES

(From the painting by George Catlin in the United States National Museum)

was then in such a state of excitement that the Indian agent rose and announced, "Hereafter on account of your rebellious attitude toward the government no annuity will be paid to the Seminoles, as heretofore."

Up to this moment Osceola had been listening with flashing eyes and compressed lips. Now he strode forward, wrapping his gay mantle close around him, over folded arms, and said scornfully:

"Neither I nor any one of my warriors care if we never receive another dollar from our Great Father!"

Then, rushing up to the table and drawing his knife, he drove it through the treaty into the table, shouting, "The only treaty I will execute is with *this!*"

So furious was his act and so passionate were his words and expression that the council hastily broke up—Indians and white men alike recognizing the tremendous force in this young brave who dared so to defy the government.

The general immediately sent word to the Secretary of War that "the Indians had positively refused to move west under the stipulations of Payne's Landing and had given as a reason that it was a white man's treaty, which they did not understand, as the interpretation of the negotiation was false," and from that time the Seminoles who hung around the fort were insolent and daring, responding to any suggestion of emigration with laughter and ridicule. At the same time it was discovered that they were buying large quantities of gunpowder and lead, and, although the officers did not take this seriously, yet, after the fact was found out, wherever and whenever they attempted to buy them it was impossible to do so. Hearing of this, Osceola, with gleaming eyes, gathered together a crowd of followers and went to a store himself to buy the desired articles.

He met with the same refusal, and with an imperious and angry gesture he exclaimed:

"Am I a negro? A slave? My skin is dark, not black. I am an Indian—a Seminole. The white man shall not make me black. I will make the white man red with blood, and then blacken him in the sun and rain, where the wolf shall smell his bones and the buzzard shall live upon his flesh!"

Conditions between the savages and the Americans were now approaching a crisis. Micanopy, himself, was old and averse to war, but he was completely under the influence of a band of young warriors of whom Osceola was the master-spirit, and they firmly refused to make any compromise with the government.

The officers became more and more incensed at this "insolence," as they called it, of the Indians, and the chiefs returned the compliment in kind. Also a crowd of speculators and adventurous whites settled on the Florida border, waiting, Sprague says, "to take possession of the Indians' land, when vacated, and to claim the negroes as slaves."

Altogether the situation was tense, but although the troops were preparing for war, they did it in a half-serious way which showed that they thought it would be only a matter of a few months to completely master the Indians, for they did not reckon with such a force as lay in the powerful personality and intelligence of young Osceola, who at that time was, we are told, "five feet eight inches tall, with a manly, frank, and open countenance, a remarkably keen, bright eye, and an independent bearing."

In Catlin's portrait of him, painted from life, the handsome young warrior wore three ostrich feathers in his black hair and a turban made of a varicolored shawl. His tunic was of gay calicoes, and he had a handsome bead sash or belt around his waist, and his rifle in his hand.

He always treated the whites with great dignity—almost amounting to insolence—and scorned the superstitions and mummeries of his race. Despite his brutality to soldiers, he was kind and thoughtful to women and children and always commanded his warriors to spare them, saying, "It is not upon them that we make war and draw the scalping-knife. It is upon men. Let us act like men."

It did not take the government long to discover who was the moving spirit of the Indian war-party, and an attempt was made to win Osceola over to a treaty of peace and submission to government wishes, but in vain. In June, 1835, General Thompson called him to a conference, but he was so daringly insolent that, secretly admiring his courage, the general ordered him under arrest; and he was put in irons, to the great consternation of his followers, who, without him, were like sheep without a shepherd.

For two days he showed the most marked humility in his imprisonment, and finally sent for a messenger to whom he said:

"Tell the general that I submit to his wishes, and will sign the treaty according to the wishes of the Great Father at Washington."

At once he was set at liberty, and, true to his promise, brought a large number of warriors to the fort, who all signed the treaty and received supplies, while General Thompson congratulated himself on having come out of a difficult situation so well, and sent full particulars of the matter to Washington; but little did either President or general know of the craft and diplomacy of intrepid young Osceola!

No sooner was he set free than by means of scouts and private messengers he sent an order with all possible haste and secrecy to every warrior of his tribe, and to all the negroes who were in sympathy with them, saying:

"Under pretense of submitting to the decree of the white men, resist and fight to the limit of your endurance!"

This command was reinforced with stirring words by which he roused his tribe to a fierce hatred of the general and the race to which he belonged, as well as to a burning desire to drive the white men out of the Seminole country, as they were trying to drive the Indians.

Osceola's eloquence and eager daring completely dominated the younger braves, who could scarcely wait now to make war on the hated pale-faces, and they hastily made Osceola war-chief of his tribe; then with craft and cunning, while apparently making ready for their journey west, moved their belongings to the depths of a great cypress swamp, where, safely intrenched on the hummocks, no white man could follow or spy on their movements.

From his own retreat in the farthest depths of the Wahoo Swamp, far beyond the prying eyes of the white man, Osceola pondered on the situation, then gave an order to kill those chiefs who had first signed the treaty—that there might be no opposition to his warlike design. In September he himself murdered one of them, and, though the deed was done in secrecy, the news of it, and of other similar acts, soon reached the whites. Frightened for their own safety, the settlers deserted their plantations and flocked to the nearest forts for protection; and the government, on the 23d of December, 1835, sent two companies of United States regulars, under Major Dade's command, to Fort King to reinforce General Thompson and subdue the Seminoles.

Osceola, from his impregnable fortress in the depths of the shadowy swamp, received the news from scouts, and a grim determination to repulse the new force was written on the features of his expressive face. He would attack this relief column before it ever reached the fort, but before doing that he would kill General Thompson, who had treated his tribe with such unkindness.

Calling together his most famous war-chiefs, he lurked for days with them in the forest near the fort, awaiting a chance to carry out his purpose, and meanwhile Dade's column was hourly coming nearer.

While awaiting his chance to make an attack, Osceola watched all movements at the fort with sharp-sighted eyes, and saw General Thompson and Lieutenant Smith saunter from the fort in the direction of a store half a mile from the garrison. In stealthy silence he and his men crept through the forest, followed the officers, and from an ambush shot and killed them in full view of the fort. Then they scalped their victims, rushed to the store, murdered the inmates, and after hastily plundering it, set fire to it, and fled to the safety of their swamp fortress.

Sprague says: "The second Seminole war was now begun in earnest. Osceola hurriedly led his warriors to the edge of Wahoo Swamp, where he had arranged to meet other chiefs and warriors, headed by old Micanopy, Jumper, and Tiger Tail. There they lurked in ambush until Major Dade's troops came in sight, when the Indians fell on them, and after a tremendous fight massacred the troops. Alligator afterward gave this account of the battle.

"So soon as all the soldiers were opposite between us and the pond," he said, "Jumper gave the whoop. Micanopy fired the first rifle, the signal agreed upon, when every Indian rose and fired, and more than half of the white men were laid on the ground dead. The soldiers' big thunder gun [cannon] was discharged several times, but the men who loaded it were shot down as soon as the smoke cleared away. The balls passed far over our heads. The soldiers shouted and whooped, the officers shook their heads and swore. There was a little man, a great brave, who shook his head at the soldiers and swore fiercely. . . . No rifle-ball could hit him. We soon came near. They had guns, but no powder. When I got inside the log pen there were three white men alive. Our negroes put them to death."

That night Osceola and his chosen men joined the warriors in a horrible celebration of their victory, the savages wearing at their belts the bloody scalps of their white victims, and gloating over the stolen stores they had obtained by the massacre. Osceola then made a wild harangue to the scalp of General Thompson, which was being carried about on a war-pole, while the head of another officer was roasting in the fire; and, ghastly as the celebration was, it was characteristic of savage warfare, and not more infamous than many a deed of the white men, whose intelligence should have made them above craft and treachery.

No sooner had Major Dade's command been wiped out than Osceola's scouts brought in tidings that General Clinch had been ordered to take the place of the murdered general, bringing with him three companies of regulars. This was news indeed! Osceola's war-like spirit thrilled at the thought of another conquest, and, calling together four hundred of his ablest warriors, with Alligator as sub-chief, he marched out of the swamp to intercept the fresh troops as they crossed the Withlachoochee River, but here General Clinch had been too clever for Osceola, having wisely taken his forces across the river in a small canoe half a mile above the regular ford, and Osceola was checkmated but undaunted.

Hiding his braves among the scrub and heavy foliage of hummocks at the river edge, he awaited developments, and at noon on the last day of December the general and his troops came past the Indian ambush, were attacked, and for an hour and a half troopers and Indians fought like demons, Osceola himself becoming the arch-fiend of the battle, while General Clinch was wary enough to imitate Indian tactics and have his men fire from behind trees or rocks or underbrush. "Osceola leaped from cover to cover, fired, then plunged from view with a yell, to seize a gun from one of his warriors and repeat one of his diabolical antics. . . . In his death-dealing dance he was the chief target of the soldiers, but no bullet seemed able to hit him, although Alligator afterward declared that the Great Chief was shot through the arm and crippled in three places, besides losing a fragment of one ear.

Inch by inch the soldiers gained ground against the savages, notwithstanding the ferocity of Osceola's attack; and at last, when a third of the red men had been disabled, General Clinch ordered an advance which drove the remaining Indians into the swamp, and Osceola saw that even the bravest of his warriors could not successfully meet the white troops when conditions were even; then, like all able generals, he at once changed his tactics to suit circumstances.

Gathering his warriors around him in his moss-hung swamp fortress, he ordered them to divide into small bands and fight a guerrilla warfare, giving direct assault only when their strength was so superior that they were certain of victory.

Immediately his braves left the swamp to do his bidding, and Osceola himself started on a series of deadly attacks on all white men who came in his path. "He would ambush troops, but after one fire and a defiant yell plunge into the deadly swamps where soldiers could never follow. Every hummock had its number of Indians and negroes carefully hidden in the dense foliage and underbrush," and, Sprague says, "woe to the express-rider, the isolated settlers, the foragers, the baggage-trains!" The savages seemed to start out of every jungle, and it was always Osceola who led them. His name became a horror to settlers and a terror to troops. "When As-se-he-ho-lar's name is whispered," said his friend Alligator, "the white man shakes with the swamp ague, and his gun drops to the ground." A terror, indeed, fell upon the whole of sunny Florida, and it became a scene of devastation and distress because of the warfare planned and carried out under the ruling spirit of young Osceola.

The War Department now took more vigorous measures to prevent further outrages, and General Gaines was sent from New Orleans with over a thousand regulars to reinforce General Clinch. He attempted to march across Florida, but unsuccessfully. Osceola attacked his troops on flank and rear, then fled, after "capturing the general's scouts, murdering his advance-guards from ambush, trapping his foragers, and sending him treacherous guides. Even the negroes used by the general as carriers betrayed his movements to Osceola," and at last, while the disheartened general was trying to transport his troops across the Withlachoochee on hastily built rafts, the savages, hidden behind dense foliage and a high embankment of sand, suddenly opened a hot fire on them from the opposite bank of the river. At once several companies were ordered to the river edge, the firing became general, and there was a brisk skirmish for an hour.

The troops then set up camp on the spot, but their guides became confused and declared that the ford was three miles farther down the river, so camp was moved to the spot indicated, but with no success; and General Gaines, believing that the time had come for an open fight with the whole body of Indians, moved camp about half a mile back from the river, on the great stretch of pine barren. Intrenched there behind a hastily built breastwork of logs, he sent a messenger to General Clinch, who was then thirty miles away at Fort Drane, advising him to cross the river ten miles up and attack the Indians both in front and rear, while he would divert their attention from this movement by seeming to cross below.

While the attack so ordered was eagerly watched for by General Gaines, the savages made constant attacks on his camp, daily setting fire to the grass, as well as to log houses and wigwams. His supplies were giving out, men were being killed constantly by the yelling mob of Indians who were always surrounding the fort, and it seemed as if relief would never come.

Time dragged on in this way until the night of March fifth, when the sentinel on guard at the fort was roused by John Cæsar, an old negro who belonged to Micanopy and was a privileged character among the Indians and his own race. After hailing the sentinel the old man passed through the encampment, shouting at the top of his voice: "The Indians are tired of fighting. They wish to come in and shake hands!"

At this joyful sound out came the general to tell him that if this were really true the Indians must come in the morning bringing a white flag, to show that their intention was genuine.

Bowing profoundly, old Cæsar turned and left camp, to bear the message to Micanopy, while the officers of the garrison awaited the morrow with high expectancy.

Noon of the following day came, and a large number of Indians were seen filing up in line back of the encampment. After some delay and many conferences with their leaders, three gaily dressed chiefs advanced to the fort, headed by

Osceola, who said that the Indians did not wish to fight any more, and were anxious to have the troops return from the Withlachoochee.

This statement was received by the general without comment, and later in the day Osceola again approached the fort and stated that Micanopy had gone away, so no treaty of peace that might be made would be binding.

In reply General Gaines said that he had no power to make such a treaty, but that if the Indians would retire to the south side of the river and remain there without troubling the inhabitants of the country, they should not be disturbed for the present, and a time and place for treating with them should be appointed.

Solemnly the warriors signified their willingness to agree to this, and so engrossed were they in the matter that not one of them saw the advance-guard of General Clinch arriving from Fort Drane and drawing up at the rear of the encampment.

General Clinch, as he approached, seeing the mass of Indians surrounding the fort and knowing nothing of the reason for the gathering, took it for granted that it boded no good; so, quickly wheeling his troops into line, he began a vigorous assault on the savages, who fled in wild confusion, and put an end to the conference.

It is said that the old negro, Cæsar, had acted without any other authority than his own impulse when he went to camp and cried out that the Indians wanted to make peace, and that when he returned and reported General Gaines's message to the Seminoles they were so angry that, but for the restraining influence of Osceola, they would have killed the old man on the spot, as his action and Osceola's acceptance of the general's invitation to a conference put an end to the plan for an attack which they had been waiting over a week to make, and by which they had hoped to break the power of the government forces.

For days they had been gathering for an assault, and great enthusiasm had prevailed among their ranks, "even decrepit men and the youngest boys taking part in the preparations for an attack, while the women on a hummock three miles distant were busy cooking provisions and running bullets for the use of the warriors"; but now General Clinch had made his unexpected assault, and the various bands melted away, dispersing to the hidden depths of the swamps, having had but two of their number killed and six wounded.

General Gaines now surrendered his command to Gen. Winfield Scott, under whose leadership, one after another, Fort King, Fort Drane, and Fort Micanopy wero given up to the Indians, until the whole southern half of Florida had fallen into the power of Osceola, who gained his victories with less than fifteen hundred warriors pitted against the United States army, whose military tactics were of no avail against the strategy of this forest leader who with his tribe could vanish in the moss-hung retreat of the great swamps to appear or to hide at will.

On went the war until fall, when General Call succeeded General Scott and promptly defeated two bands of Seminoles, so regaining part of the lost country. But the Indians were still hidden in the Wahoo Swamp, Osceola's headquarters, and in a determination to achieve greater results General Jesup was sent to take General Call's place. The new commander of the American forces brought with him eight thousand troops, and bloodhounds from Cuba to track the Indians to their swamp retreats, but the dogs, having been trained to trail negroes only, were useless to Jesup, and he at once planned and carried out a new and different campaign from that of his predecessors.

He offered the Indians pardon and comradeship, and a few bands accepted his overtures, but as soon as they had been well fed and had obtained valuable information about the movements of the troops, they fled to tell Osceola what they had heard. Jesup was baffled in his scheme, and at no time could he form any correct idea of the number of savages fighting against his troops, for, pursued, the Seminoles were always swallowed up by the great, gloomy swamps; fleeing from the soldiers, they disappeared among the Everglades only to reappear a stronger and more desperate band.

In the depths of the cypress swamp lay the Indians' council-ground, near which lived many of the most noted chiefs, and trails or footpaths communicated with all their hiding-places, though no trail whatever could be seen outside the swamp, as such would guide their pursuers. In the swamp lay many islands and hiding-places inaccessible to the feet of the white man, but on which the Indians lay concealed for days and weeks at a time.

Thus the Seminoles were able from their fortress to continue the war against their bitter foes, and month after month evaded the American soldiers with supreme strategy. By the light of a glimmering moon, or again, in the full glare of the tropical sun, Osceola was more than once joined by bold pirates of the surrounding sea, who in Indian disguise came to shore and fought by the side of the young war-chief, whose craft and cunning were those of the jungle, but whose intelligence was worthy of a white general.

Not only was Osceola a fierce savage, he was a commander who was superbly scornful in his dignity of office, and once, when facing a captured officer and holding the loot which had been taken from him, he suddenly flung the coin in the American's face, hissing: "Money! 'Tis coined from the red man's blood!"

"From time to time he was joined by bands of Creeks from Georgia, as well as by those occasional sea-pirates who attached themselves to his following, but never did he have more than two thousand warriors with him to fight against the large number of American troops." Still "the debilitating climate, the treacherous swamps, the white man's ignorance of the jungle, together with the activity and skill of Osceola, continued to outwit the ablest generals," while "the savages continued to suddenly assemble in force at some weak point, strike a fatal blow, and then scatter into parties to their hiding-places without leaving a trace behind."

But there was so much suffering among the Indians that old Micanopy became disheartened, and, taking with him four other chiefs as old and despondent as himself, and three hundred loyal warriors, he went to General Jesup's camp and officially surrendered the whole nation.

The general joyfully accepted the surrender, and immediately sent word to Washington that the Seminoles were subdued. Osceola, who had been out reconnoitering, returned to Wahoo Swamp to hear of this act of his veteran chiefs; and, retiring to the depths of his jungle abode, he pondered long and deeply on his next move.

Some hours later an unknown Indian in the dress of a forest vagabond sauntered into the magic circle of the none too carefully guarded camp of those Indians who had earlier in the day surrendered with Micanopy. Suddenly flinging off his disguise and waving his arms in a compelling gesture, he cried, "I am Osceola! Take back the treaty of peace you made to-day!"

So strong was his influence over the Seminoles, young and old, that before the night was over every brave had stampeded the jungle, and the general's short-lived triumph was at an end.

But though they were for the most part undaunted, still on the war-path, Osceola's followers were now suffering frightfully from famine, which was slowly depleting their forces. Then came the worst blow of all—the supply of powder was short! At this news even Osceola's superb courage gave way, and with a tragic gesture he cried out: "I cannot make powder. If the Great Spirit will show me how, I will dye the land he has given us with the blood of the white man until it is red like the sunset sky."

A crisis had come. Gathering around their commander, the faint-hearted warriors begged Osceola to open peace negotiations with General Hernandez, who was now in command of that part of the army in Florida east of the St. Johns River. Osceola quickly responded to their desire and agreed to open communications with Hernandez, who was at that time conducting a series of vigorous measures along the Atlantic coast south of St. Augustine.

"On the 9th of September Hernandez with his men assaulted the camp of King Philip, a famous Seminole chief, and took him and eleven of his tribe prisoners. On the following day he attacked the camp of the chief Uchee Billy, and secured him, his brother Uchee Jack, and eighteen men." This led to the surrender of the son of King Philip, Coacoochee, who had previously received a message from his father asking him to come and see him. As he went to the enemy's camp at his father's request, and as Osceola's messenger to General Hernandez, Coacoochee was sure that he would not be held as a prisoner, and went fearlessly, carrying with him from the general to Osceola a white plume and a "neatly wrought bead pipe," which was sent to signify that "the path was white and safe."

With Coacoochee went Blue Snake, who was also a messenger and also carried a white plume and a message from Cao-hoje, another influential chief.

General Hernandez received the chiefs graciously, and, after consulting General Jesup, sent Coacoochee back to tell Osceola that he would grant a conference with the Seminoles, but on the clear understanding that it would be to make arrangements for their emigration to the west.

Away went Coacoochee carrying his message, and back he came on an appointed day to state that Osceola and Cao-hoje, with one hundred warriors, had already started toward St. Augustine to confer with General Hernandez. Eager to hasten their coming, Hernandez, with a small detail of soldiers, went to meet the Indians, carrying supplies for them; and about twenty miles south, at Pelican's Creek, he met an advance-party headed by John Cavallo, who told him that Osceola was expected to join the party that evening. Leaving the provisions he had brought, the general went back to the fort after telling the savages to choose their own position near the garrison when Osceola arrived, and to let him know of the event, that he might hold the expected conference with them.

That night Osceola and Cao-hoje marched up and joined the advance-party, and, as the general had promised, word being brought to him of their arrival, he met them with his own staff and a portion of General Jesup's.

Then facing the proud leader of the Seminoles, Hernandez asked, "What is the object of the Indians in coming in at this time? Are they prepared to deliver up the negroes taken from the citizens, at once? Why have they not surrendered them already, as promised by Cao-hoje at Fort King?" These and other questions were put to the Seminole leader, the last questions being these: "Have the principal chiefs, Micanopy, Jumper, Cloud, and Alligator, sent a messenger, and, if so, what is their message? Why have not these chiefs come in themselves?"

To the first few questions Osceola answered promptly, and it was evident that the Indians were willing to surrender the negroes they had taken during the war; but whether because the other questions roused a suspicion in Osceola's mind, or because he knew that the large part of his tribe were still unwilling to emigrate and were going to be forced to do so, cannot be said, but the great Chief became evasive, then silent, and finally, turning to Cao-hoje, said in a low voice, "I feel choked; you must speak for me"—a proof of genuine emotion rare among his race.

The general was at first mystified, then suspicious at his conduct, and at last decided to take no chances, in the face of General Jesup's command—"Let the chiefs and warriors know that we have been deceived by them long enough. Order the whole party directly to town. . . . They must move instantly. . . ."

Watching Osceola closely, he determined to make the most of a rare opportunity, and to arrest the young war-chief on the spot. He gave a signal, and the trooper closed around the Indians, taking them prisoners. The arms, baggage, and ponies were collected, and the line of march was taken up to St. Augustine.

Osceola, daring, intrepid Osceola, had been captured, under a flag of truce, by a trick of the white men whom he had so long evaded in legitimate warfare. His enemy had done what under the most extenuating circumstances is not easy to condone in the commander of civilized troops; and, worn out from months of the hardest kind of fighting and broken in spirit by the injustice done him, Osceola was taken to the St. Augustine prison. Coacoochee was taken, too, but contrived to escape through the loophole of a casement in the fort where he slept. Hastily he fled to the south, and succeeded in reaching a Seminole camp, when the band were on their way to meet and treat with General Jesup.

In burning words caused by his anger and resentment Coacoochee told of his capture and imprisonment and the treatment he and the other Indians had received, and his listeners became so enraged that instead of surrendering, as they had intended to do, they immediately gave up the idea, and not only did not further communicate with the American generals, but, retiring again to their fortress, continued the war which the commanding officers of the army had hoped to terminate.

Osceola meanwhile had been transferred to Fort Moultrie, near Charleston, "where his proud stoicism and haughty courage dropped from him like an outworn garment."

Had he been defeated in open combat his Indian spirit would have accepted the defeat, but to have been tricked into capture by the duplicity of the white men in a moment when he trusted them was beyond his endurance. The gallant young chief became so melancholy that it was impossible to rouse his interest even for a moment. He refused even to see his friends, and when his loyal followers approached him with a petition that he emigrate with the other Seminoles and make the best of the situation, as they might have to do, the plea was useless. He maintained a haughty silence and an impenetrable reserve which showed that imprisonment and capture had struck a death-blow to his proud spirit.

He became an object of general interest to the officers of the garrison, who were so sympathetic with the brilliant young prisoner that if they could have had their way he would have gone free; but instead, a captive, he became seriously ill of throat trouble—refused food and drink, and was soon found to be dying.

Dr. Weedon, who was with him at the end, has given this account of his last moments:

> About half an hour before he died he seemed to be sensible that he was dying, and, although he could not speak, he signified by signs that he wished me to send for his chiefs, and for the officers of the post, whom I called in. He made signs to his wives (of whom he had two, and also two fine little children by his side) to go and bring his full dress which he wore in time of war; which having been brought in, he rose up in his bed, which was on the floor, and put on his shirt, his leggings and moccasins, girded on his war-belt, his bullet-pouch and powder-horn, and laid his knife by the side of him, on the floor. He then called for his red paint and his looking-glass, which was held before him, when he deliberately painted one half of his face, his neck, his throat, his wrists, the back of his hands, and the handle of his knife red, . . . a custom practised when the irrevocable oath of war is taken. His knife he then placed in its sheath under his belt, and he carefully arranged his turban on his head, and his three ostrich plumes that he was in the habit of wearing in it. Being thus prepared in full dress, he lay down for a few minutes to recover strength sufficient, when he rose up as before, and with most benignant and pleasing smiles extended his hand to me and to all of the officers and chiefs that were around him, and shook hands with us all in dead silence, and also with his wives and his little children. He made a signal for them to lower him down upon his bed, which was done, and he then drew slowly from his belt his scalping-knife, which he firmly grasped in his right hand, laying it across the other, on his breast, and in a moment smiled away his last breath without a struggle or a groan.

So passed away Osceola, the brilliant young war-chief who by his masterly strategy had defeated the ablest generals of his day and led his people in a costly and disastrous five-years war.

SEQUOYAH

SEQUOYAH: THE CHEROKEE CADMUS

THE mountainous country where Georgia, Tennessee, and North Carolina touch. A Cherokee log house at the edge of the forest, with its guardian giants of the woods, and Sequoyah at work!

In a little clearing at the rear of the log house, with his supply of charcoal, wrapping-paper, and "talking-leaves" spread out before him, sat Sequoyah, where he had worked through long days and weeks, and where he was often still to be found, rapt in thought, when evening shadows fell across the great mountain peaks towering behind him and mists of oncoming night enveloped the peaceful valley beyond.

And why was he here—this Cherokee, who by custom of his race and tribe should have been absorbed in chase or hunt, or waging war upon those invading settlers who were crowding into the Indian country of the eastern mountaineers?

Let history tell its story from an earlier time when, in the latter part of the eighteenth century, on a certain day Indian met Indian, and with signs and nods showed approval of an order of their venerable chief, Atakullakulla, that there should be a dance that night in recognition of the achievement of the young lad, Sikwayi, or Sequoyah, son of the Cherokee woman whose father was a chief of Echota.

Sequoyah was as lithe of limb and sturdy of body as any of his other bronze-skinned, black-eyed Indian comrades, but even as a very young boy his tastes were not the same as theirs. While they roamed the forests, hunting, fishing, or swimming in the clear mountain streams, Sequoyah, heedless of their pleading, would shake his head and remain behind alone, building miniature models of such houses as those in which the Cherokee mountaineers lived, using small sticks for uprights and the bark of trees to cover the rounding roof and sides, as was done in the larger ones he was copying.

Not satisfied with work on such a small scale, he then began to construct a real shed to be used as a dairy, where the few cows which his mother owned could be housed and the milk properly cared for. By the time this was finished and in use Sequoyah was fifteen years old and ready to "make his medicine," as was the custom of every Indian boy growing into manhood.

Wandering away from home, he spent a couple of days lying on the ground in a remote corner of the forest, crying to the Great Spirit—reverence for whom is co-existent with life itself in the Indian's breast—and fasting. At last, in spite of hunger and fear, he fell asleep and dreamed that a toad hopped into a fold of his garment, which was the Great Spirit's sign that the little animal was to be his mysterious protector throughout his life, and even after death. His "medicine" made, he rose and returned home, carrying with him a real toad, the skin of which he made into what was called a "medicine-bag" by stuffing it with dried grass and herbs—and always afterward he carried this in some fold of his clothing to protect him from harm.

Having "made his medicine," he was now ready to take his place among the young warriors of the tribe; but as combat of any kind was distasteful to him, he turned his attention to the "picture-writing" of his people, who, having no

SEQUOYAH: THE CHEROKEE CADMUS

alphabet such as the more fortunate white man possessed, were obliged to express their thoughts and ideas in rude sketches made on wood or bark or stone or the skins of animals.

Though an untaught Cherokee, ignorant of any language but that of his tribe, Sequoyah was thrown into daily contact with English colonists and fur-traders who were now swarming into the Indians' territory; and, seeing their use of the "talking-leaves," as the Indian called the white man's printed page, Sequoyah became keen to express in the Cherokee way fancies and facts as clearly for his tribe as the white men did for their people. At first he cut the mark of his tribe or clan on rocks and trees as he went about the country; then he began to paint at home on bark or skins, and became so skilful in his art that daily a crowd of spectators gathered around him, watching men and animals, warriors and chiefs, grow under his clever fingers.

With charcoal and red ocher and varicolored dyes extracted from the roots of plants for the purpose, he depicted such mighty deeds as he heard the chiefs relate nightly before the camp-fire, and common scenes of the Indian boy's life in the open, or such exploits as he himself dreamed some day of achieving.

Then he undertook a more important piece of work, a ceremonial robe, which at last was finished. Of softest deerskin it was made, hanging from the shoulders in the loose, straight fashion of such garments. On one side the sign of the bear, his mother's clan, was painted between the shoulders, and on the other, in red and black characters, was a tale of battle in which Cherokee warriors figured prominently.

The robe was done, and Atakullakulla had ordered a

dance in honor of the boy whose ability was acknowledged by all, and held in superstitious awe by many, who felt that either the Great Spirit or the powers of darkness must have had a hand in creating such work—and who could say which?

It was the hour for the dance, and by mountain trail and valley road and from every Cherokee habitation dotted over the hillside came warriors and women to an open space, used almost nightly for dancing. Not a warrior of the tribe was absent, and Sequoyah was a conspicuous feature in the foreground of the crowd.

In the flare of many torches the brilliantly painted faces and elaborately stained bodies of the warriors shone in glistening gaiety, while their ears, slit and stretched to an enormous size, according to the habit of the tribe, did not add to their beauty; but the women, with their flowing black hair and gaily beaded garments, were taller and finer-looking than the men, as they moved among the crowd with lithe dignity and grace.

All was ready. The monotonous music of drum and rattle began, then stopped. From the crowd, his tomahawk whirling above his head, a warrior sprang to the central cleared space and hopped and danced and capered to the fantastic rhythm of drum and rattle, then gave a blood-curdling whoop. The music stopped again; the torches flared. Assuming a dramatic pose, the hero began a stirring tale of the taking of his first scalp; then, pulling from his belt a string of wampum, he threw it carelessly on a huge bearskin spread for the purpose at his feet. Again the music, the dancing, the tale of mighty deeds. Then he sprang back into the crowd, and another warrior jumped forward to whoop and dance and pose and throw his present on the bearskin; and this went on until every man there had told his tale and thrown his offering on the skin. The music then stopped playing while the gifts were counted and divided between the musicians and Sequoyah, the hero of the dance, who, as the sun rose over the hills, bore home a heavy offering of paint, wire, arrow-heads, and, best of all, wampum, the Indian money, of which there was a small gourd full.

Having won such a triumph and done such a large piece of picture-writing Sequoyah was no longer willing to make use of smaller surface for his work, but it was not easy to obtain buffalo-hides or deerskins, as those who secured them in hunting bartered them to the English for the commodities of life; so Sequoyah took his bow and went into the forest to secure for himself the coveted material.

Quick of eye and sure of foot as an Indian youth should be, in the swift pursuit of a fleeting stag he crept down a steep incline heedless that the earth had been loosened by a storm; he slipped with the sliding ground, a rock fell, pinning him under its huge surface, and for a full hour he lay writhing in its giant grip before he was found and extricated. Two stalwart Indians carried him home, and then followed long weeks of torture, during which he suffered as only a wild creature in captivity can suffer. Roots and herbs were first tried, but failed to allay the agony in his back, the tribal medicine was administered without success, and as a final resort a mystery or medicine man, was called. He inquired carefully into Sequoyah's symptoms, dreams, and sins, and announced that he would attempt a cure of the young patient. The news spread rapidly, and several hundred spectators, including Indians and traders, gathered as if by magic to see the trial made.

The man of mystery gave his commands. The crowd must form a ring around Sequoyah, who lay on a mattress of boughs. There must be space left around him for any necessary operations to take place, and an opening must be left through the crowd wide enough for the healer to pass through without touching any one, a very necessary part of the ceremony.

The commands having been obeyed, there was a murmur of "Hush-sh-sh-sh! he is coming!" followed by a deathlike stillness.

Softly the medicine-man crept up the aisle opened for him through the crowd; there was no noise of his stealthy footsteps, no sound except the tinkling of ornaments on his dress. Slowly, silently; crouching, he crept into the ring with a slow, tilting step, swaying to one side and the other, his body and head covered entirely with the skin of a yellow bear, the head of which (his own being inside) served as a mask. In one hand he shook a huge rattle and with the other brandished his magic medicine-wand. Then, dancing and pawing and jumping around Sequoyah, he yelped and howled and growled and grunted and snarled, muttering an incantation to both good and bad spirits, while he clapped a paw on various parts of Sequoyah's back, moistening it with saliva now and again. For half an hour this strange operation was kept up, the audience remaining in awed silence. No sign of change or relief was visible on Sequoyah's face. The healer stopped for a moment with arms outstretched like wings, viewing his prostrate patient; then with a sudden whoop he dashed through the crowd and disappeared, though Sequoyah's pain was unrelieved.

The supreme arts of medicine and mystery having been put to the test and failed, there was nothing further to try, and Sequoyah was obliged to make the best of his limitations, to bear the pain, which gradually lessened; and, though he was never again able to hunt or swim or run, yet as time wore on he was able to take his place among the men of his tribe, and the disability gave him only a passing regret, for it served as a greater excuse for turning his attention in a more pleasing direction than that of physical exercise.

While he had been so absorbed in "picture-writing" before his accident, he had felt a keen desire to create objects of artistic beauty, and now at a rude forge, hastily constructed for the purpose, he began to make the silver ornaments so universally worn by both Indian men and women.

His experiments were successful beyond his wildest hopes, and when he showed the first armlets, ear-rings, and brooches of his own designing, those who saw them hastily spread the news of Sequoyah's new achievement. At once he became a most popular person, especially with the Indian maidens, who daily visited the forge, and many a smile was flashed from black-eyed beauties in exchange for coveted trinkets, while Sequoyah grew daily more susceptible to the flattery they gave him. One dark-skinned young girl of his own clan, as shy as a deer and as beautiful as the sunrise, in her soft skin garment, with its gay bead-work, so pierced the young artist's heart with the arrow of her intense admiration that, after offering her his most elaborate designs for a mere smile, he added his heart, and the bargain was concluded—the marriage arranged.

Because of the novelty of Sequoyah's designs and the perfection of their execution they were in great demand as well by the traders and settlers as by the Indians, and money and praise flowed in fast; but in a sudden reaction—for his temperament was one of moods—he cast aside his artistic work for the making of hoes and rakes and spades. These were so much more practical in design than any others, that English and Cherokee, colonist and settler, at once eagerly bought and put them into use; and, wishing to have the credit of his superior workmanship, Sequoyah asked a friendly white man to put his name on a piece of paper. This Mr. Lowrey did, using Sequoyah's English name, George Guess, and from it Sequoyah made a die with which from that day every article made by him was stamped.

But success with its accompaniment of money and popularity did Sequoyah great injury. Seeing his fascination for the girls, the young Indian braves also flocked to his forge to admire his work; and Sequoyah, with true Indian hospitality, responded to their admiration by lavish entertaining of a different kind from that of an earlier day, when the Cherokee "treated" with game and sweet-potatoes. Instead, Sequoyah would buy a keg of the white man's rum —alas, for that evil habit of the Indian the white man alone stands responsible—and with a party of his boon companions and flatterers would retire to the woods, there to remain until the keg was empty and the effects of the debauch had worn off. This occurred so often that his supply of money ran low, the forge was unused, his pretty squaw was neglected, and he himself was fast losing his remarkable ability in handicraft, when his weakness became common talk among the white men, to whom the talented young Indian was an object of keen interest. Then Mr. Lowrey, always Sequoyah's good friend, resolved to make a great effort to save the young man from his evil habits. Plunging boldly into the forest, he found Sequoyah and four comrades, all in a heavy stupor, and carried off the unresisting artist to his own log house, where, as soon as the effects of the rum had worn off enough to leave Sequoyah clear-headed again, he spoke to him in cleverly calculated words of the commercial value of the talent he was ruining and his great importance in his tribe and clan.

Gravely Sequoyah listened, gravely he gripped Mr. Lowrey's hand, and, nodding, spoke of his determination to give up the "fire-water" and all that it led to. And he was as good as his word.

Breaking away from the seductive band of flatterers, he started his forge again, made peace with his little wife, and began to spend his leisure hours with the older and wiser men of the tribe, whose discussions were of serious matters and from whom he could gain much valuable information. Among them he heard many conversations concerning the magic power possessed by the white man of making curious marks on paper, such as those in which Mr. Lowrey had written his name, which meant the same thing to every white man, unlike the picture-writing of the Indian, which meant this or that according to the imagination of those who examined it. Some spoke of this power of the white man reverently as a gift of the Great Spirit, while others, less reverent and more superstitious, characterized it as sorcery or a clever trick. Sequoyah alone pronounced it an art which could be practised by red men as well as white if they only had the ingenuity. Something of equal value to the Indian he, Sequoyah, could and would invent for the Cherokee. He spoke confidently of his ability to "talk on paper," but those who heard the statement only laughed in his face and paid no attention to his assertion. As in his other achievements, however, he was too deeply interested to heed their ridicule or incredulity. From the days of his early picture-writing he had felt awe for the civilization and education of the white man — now he was going to probe into its causes and educate his tribe, if that were possible.

Gathering together a large number of thin birchwood sheets, on each one with infinite care and labor he painted a picture representing the name of some natural object. The process took a long time and was so difficult that he was obliged to give it up as useless when he found that he had accumulated a number of characters greater than he could remember, while the vocabulary of the language was still far from complete.

But this did not discourage him; in fact, his interest was always keener in any line of work which presented difficulties to solve, and he began again. Trading some silver ornaments for sheets of wrapping-paper, he bound them with thongs of deerskin into a rough book, and began another series of experiments, helped now by some torn leaves out of an old English spelling-book which he bartered from a fur-trader. He could not read a word on the "talking leaves," as he called the pages, but he saw that they were covered with figures of distinct shape, such figures as he was taxing his brain to invent for his own Cherokee alphabet. Some of the English characters he copied, and adopted for his work, pronouncing them in an entirely different way from that used in our English alphabet. For example, he appropriated the letters W, H, and B, but W stands for the sound *la* and the others for sounds just as far from their English equivalents.

Patiently, laboriously, he worked on, trying to gather some idea from the English pages from which to construct his own system of characters and words, and finally concluded that as there were eighty-six syllables in Cherokee, he would make a series of eighty-six characters to represent them, and by study found that these characters could be so combined as to represent every word in the Cherokee dialect. This discovery brought with it not only elation, but suspense, for who could yet say whether he could work it out to a practical result or not?

On he toiled through two years, so absorbed in perfecting his system that not only were wife, forge, and comrades neglected, but he was oblivious to the encroachments of white settlers upon lands which had been reserved for the Cherokees by treaty with the government, whose bad faith now obliged the tribe to cede away tract after tract of their most valuable property. There was, therefore, warfare constant and bitter between the Cherokees, the State of Georgia, and the United States government; and the Cherokees were fiercely resisting the determined effort of the government to let in the white man and drive the Indian of the southern Alleghanies beyond the Mississippi River. There some of the tribe, worn out with their unequal struggle with more civilized powers, had already settled in Arkansas and were forming a new community on the large tract of land allotted them by the government.

But to this sad condition of affairs Sequoyah was indifferent, so long as his work was not interrupted. Daily he was to be found in the clearing behind his log house, careless of incredulity or disapproval, absorbed in thought and study from dawn until darkness fell. Then, rousing at the touch of a small hand, he would answer the appeal of his six-year-old daughter, reluctantly follow her to the house for the evening meal, and later enjoy the flickering glow of the camp-fire with family and friends—but with his thought constantly on the subject nearest his heart.

At last the eighty-six characters of his alphabet were achieved. Now for a proof of its value!

Calling his little girl to his side, he taught her the first character, then another and another, persisting day by day until she had learned the entire alphabet. Then he asked her to write one word and a second and third at his dictation. The test was satisfactory! She could write and read correctly any word he asked for, by combining the characters according to the sound of the word required. Now to show his people the wonderful achievement and prove its value to the nation!

But this was not so easy a task. Even Mr. Lowrey was so skeptical of the Cherokee's ability to create an alphabet that he put off the test of it week after week, despite Sequoyah's pleading. At last, merely from a good-natured desire to please the eager Indian, Mr. Lowrey went to his log house to see the great invention put to the proof.

Gleefully Sequoyah asked him to dictate several words and sentences, which he wrote down in the Cherokee characters. Then, calling his little girl from her play, he showed her what he had written, and without hesitation or difficulty she read the sentences. Greatly interested now, Mr. Lowrey himself sent her away and dictated more sentences, even a short story, and every time the child read what was written quickly and easily. This was remarkable. Grasping Sequoyah's hand, Mr. Lowrey expressed his intense interest and surprise in what Sequoyah had achieved, and promised to help him gain recognition of his work.

But here again came a period of weary waiting, for any mention of the subject to a Cherokee was met by a shake of the head and the exclamation "Poor old Sequoyah!" There was prejudice against the ways of the white man to contend with, distrust of anything so alien to the custom of the tribe, and an intense fear of sorcery, and it took ten long years to convince the Cherokees that there might be something of value to the nation in this achievement of Sequoyah's, and he was a man full fifty years old when the head chiefs of the tribe at last consented to a public test of the new alphabet. Accordingly, a number of the most intelligent young men of the tribe were asked to place themselves under Sequoyah's tuition that they might give a trial to this invention which was so much talked about by Mr. Lowrey. For three days the new scholars were absent from dance and hunt, then, having learned the alphabet, were called before a body of judges chosen for the purpose, and in the presence of an immense crowd of spectators wrote and read sentences dictated either by one of the judges or by one of the excited audience.

It was the supreme moment of Sequoyah's life. The chorus of applause swelled to a huge volume of sound; a murmur of admiration rose from every mouth, while scores of upturned faces expressed not only surprise but awe that one of their own people had been able to achieve this thing for his tribe. What more could Sequoyah ask than this?

Once aroused, public interest rose to a flood-tide of enthusiasm, and so many students flocked about "The Master," as he was now called, that he could not teach them all. The boys and young warriors of the tribe, catching the fever from those first pupils, were all seized with a mad desire for lessons in the new art of writing and reading, for the speedy ability to make use of Sequoyah's "talking-leaves," and the older men of the tribe began to grumble over the enchantment which was making the young forgetful of warfare, chase, and dance, while they spent their time poring over bits of paper. But the objections of age could not overcome the enthusiasm of youth, and the progressive party had its way. Schools were opened, text-books were compiled, and Sequoyah thrilled with joy over the results of his labor and the honors paid to him.

However, neither the achievement or its flattering results turned his head, as success used to do. This he took seriously, and his one thought was to spread his wonderful invention wherever there was a Cherokee to profit by it. Part of his tribe had already settled in Arkansas—to Arkansas he would go with his precious gift of an alphabet.

His arrival there made a stir in the new colony, and there was intense excitement when, gathering the settlers together in a public place, he told them the story of his invention and the marvelous results of its use. Then he invited pupils to test its worth, and there was the same public trial and public acclaim as in Georgia over this system which raised the Cherokee to a footing with the white man. Almost every warrior in the settlement placed himself under Sequoyah's tuition, and he taught diligently until he saw the results for which he had been watching. Then the time had come for him to go back to Georgia. When he announced this intention there was a chorus of protests, but the firmness of his resolve allowed of no alternative, and so he was allowed to go, after he had promised to correspond with his new pupils, which promise he faithfully kept, although this use of the Cherokee "talking-leaves" to send news from such a distance caused some superstitious persons to malign both teacher and pupils.

Full of elation that he had been able to spread education among his people, he journeyed back to Georgia; but even with his knowledge of what he had achieved, on his return he was completely unprepared to receive an invitation to a public gathering in his own honor, and still more so when, with appropriate ceremonies, he was presented with a silver medal in recognition of his valuable service to his tribe. With great solemnity the medal was suspended around Sequoyah's neck, and he wore it always afterward, exhibiting it with the greatest pride.

No sooner had he settled in his old home than pupils

flocked around him again, begging for instruction, and for almost a year every hour of his days was filled with teaching; but the constant warfare between the government, the invading settlers, and his tribe became so distasteful to him that he again said farewell to his old comrades and returned to Arkansas, where he settled permanently, becoming a prominent feature in the community; and soon he had the extreme satisfaction of reading parts of the Bible translated into Cherokee by means of his alphabet, and also, in 1828, of seeing *The Phœnix*, the first newspaper printed in English and Cherokee, successfully issued.

In that same year Sequoyah, now a man of dignified bearing and of a polished manner, was sent to Washington as an envoy of the Arkansas band in whose affairs he played such a conspicuous part, and both the trip and his interviews with the "Great Father" and other statesmen were a keen satisfaction to the quick-minded Indian, who was able later to put into practice several ideas which he gained in Washington.

Ten years went by, and when the march of civilization drove the remaining eastern Cherokees to join the western settlement, they found their old comrade exerting a marked influence in the Arkansas community, and he continued to be a powerful factor in the reunited nation.

But intoxicating as power is to a man of Sequoyah's temperament, yet, as of old, speculative ideals were always more important to him than the more practical ones of politics and society, and the desire to further extend the knowledge of his alphabet possessed him.

From the moment when he heard that a lost tribe of the Cherokees were supposed to be living in the still more remote West, to go in search of them with his precious gift became his dominant idea, and he laid his project before the nation, with an appeal for an annuity equal to the salary of a chief, to support him during his trip to the Far West for the furtherance of education among his people.

The plea was granted, and Sequoyah, now over seventy years old, gleefully fitted up a prairie-wagon with camp equipment, and also with books and writing-materials—in fact, with everything needed for the instructing of those who might desire to be taught.

Then he started out, journeying across the mountains and prairies in search of New Mexico and the missing tribe. His granddaughter, who saw the expedition start, has written an account of it.

She says:

> I remember well the morning they left. His son, Teece, and several other men—I do not know their names—went with him. He limped a little as he walked, and coughed a great deal. It was said that he had the breast complaint. His friends thought a change of climate would help him. I was present when the men returned and reported his death.
>
> They told how his health began to improve until after passing Grand River. Then they found only bad water; . . . the provisions became scarce and they depended entirely on game. It seemed that there was nothing for them. One of the men always stayed with Sequoyah until at last he sent them all to hunt. They remained overnight, and on their return to the place next day where they had left him, he was gone, but had left directions for them to follow him to another place which he described.
>
> They hurried on, but found him dead. They put his papers with his body and wrapped it with blankets and put it away upon a kind of shelf in a small cave where nothing could disturb it. They said they marked the place so they could find it, but the men sent to bring the body failed to find the place.

Indomitable Sequoyah! His final resting-place may be unmarked, but his lasting monument is that gift to his people which lifted them from barbarism into a place among the civilized nations of the world. The pages of history are filled with names of Indians who did mighty deeds of valor, from whose belts hang the scalp-locks of unnumbered victims, and in whose strong right arms lies the secret of their supremacy. From the time of Red Jacket, the orator of the Senecas, to the great Sitting Bull of our own time, there is a long line of Indian prophets who forecast and inveigh against the white man's supremacy in words of burning eloquence; there are chiefs and warriors whose prowess in war has been chronicled over and over again, but fitting tribute has never been paid to Sequoyah, keen-eyed, far-sighted, with the vision of such priceless worth to his people.

Crippled in body, but strong in mind and inspiration, he stands alone, unique, among the Cherokees of Georgia, the Cadmus of his tribe.

KING PHILIP

KING PHILIP: HERO OF THE WAMPANOAGS

THAT was a strange gathering on the 11th of April, 1671, in the little meeting-house at Taunton, Massachusetts, when Puritans and savages were awaiting the conference for which they had been called together.

Fierce Indian braves, armed and painted as if for war, wrapped in the gayest of mantles, their flowing black hair decorated with sweeping plumes and fantastic head-dresses, were in marked contrast to the austere Puritans who sat on the opposite side of the meeting-house, in plain black garb, with close-cut hair and portentously long faces. Facing Puritans and savages before the rude pulpit of the place of worship were ranged three stern Massachusetts commissioners, sent by the governor as umpires of this conference which had been called at the demand of the Plymouth colony.

The reason for this leads us back to the time when Massasoit, the revered old chieftain of the Wampanoags, died, leaving two sons, Wamsutta, or Alexander, as the English named him, who succeeded his father as chief of the tribe, and Pometacom, or Philip, who in his turn came to the Indian throne when Alexander died, poisoned by the English, so his wife and subjects believed. Really, he was the victim of a broken heart because of the indignity offered him when he was arrested and taken by force to Plymouth to answer to a charge of plotting against the colonists.

This so broke Alexander's proud spirit that on the way

to Plymouth he was found to be dying, and his escort, mooring their canoes by the river edge, landed and placed him on a grassy mound under an overarching tree. There, with his warriors gathered around him and his head pillowed in the lap of his beautiful and devoted wife, Wetamoo, he died, leaving such a fire of revenge in the heart of Wetamoo as was later to flame into disaster for the race she held responsible for her husband's death. By birth Wetamoo was a princess of the Pocasset tribe, and could command several hundred warriors if she so desired, so in her the new king, Philip, would have a valuable ally if he went to war against the English.

Philip, "broad-browed and noble-minded," was an Indian of superior mind as well as of superb physical endowment when he became monarch of the Wampanoags. He knew only too well the power of the English and the danger to be faced in declaring war against them, remembering the fatal termination of the Pequot War; yet he saw with equal plainness that unless the encroachments of the English could be stopped his own race was doomed.

In his father's day the power of the Wampanoags, because of the mental and military ability of their leader, had extended over more than thirty tribes in Rhode Island and Massachusetts. But, though they were a powerful forest nation, they were a peaceful one, as for forty years they had not waged war against the English or any other tribe. Now, however, Philip foresaw that war must soon come if he were to protect his people from destruction; but with the caution of a born general he determined to wait until he had good reason for action before striking a blow at the colonists.

The new king of the Wampanoags took up his residence at Pokanoket, or Mount Hope, which had been the principal settlement of the tribe since Massasoit's time. The famous hill is on the east side of Narragansett Bay, on the Bristol peninsula, and had been selected by the veteran Indian king for his royal headquarters because of its extensive view of far-reaching forests and wide indented bays. Massasoit's residence had been a rough lodge in a clearing of the forest, but King Philip erected a more elaborate building of logs and bark for his own use, while the lodges of his chiefs were scattered over the surrounding acres of woodland to the edge of a great swamp near by.

There, at Mount Hope, for nine long years Philip lived in retirement, waiting for his hour to come; and while he waited Indians and colonists became more exasperated against one another, for deeds of violence were committed constantly on both sides; but Philip was not yet ready to make a move, being still busy with completing his plan for an alliance of all the New England tribes, except the Mohegans, who were loyal allies of the English.

At one time during those years of waiting Philip was strongly drawn toward the religion taught by Christian missionaries, but he was quick-witted enough to realize that with the introduction of Christianity all the manners and customs peculiar to his people must give way to those of civilized nations, and so he became bitterly opposed to the strange religion.

At another time, having heard that a Christian Indian named Assassamooyh (called by the English John Gibbs) had spoken disrespectfully of his father, Massasoit, Philip started off to track down the offender, for whose lack of reverence, according to the Indian code, he should instantly forfeit his life at the hands of the nearest relative of the slandered one.

Assassamooyh was discovered in the house of a colonist on the island of Nantucket, and there went Philip in hot haste. A messenger ran in to Assassamooyh and announced breathlessly, "Pometacom is here!" Jumping up, Assassamooyh rushed from the door, with Philip at his heels. From house to house the frightened Indian ran, followed by Philip brandishing his tomahawk. On went the pursuer and pursued until they came to a high bank. Down leaped Assassamooyh and vanished in the depths of the forest, while Philip returned to the shore and paddled away in his canoe, feeling that the insult to his father's memory had been suitably avenged, even though he had not killed the traitor.

It was now the eighth year of Philip's reign over the Wampanoags, and there were persistent rumors of war among the four colonies of New England, although there were no positive facts to confirm the rumors. But still they spread. A superstitious colonist studying the heavens on a clear night declared he saw an Indian bow and arrow outlined against the sky; again, an Indian scalp was seen silhouetted against the disk of an eclipse of the moon. It was said that the northern lights were ominously bright, that troops of phantom horsemen could be heard dashing through the air by sensitive ears, the sighing of the night wind was like the sound of whistling bullets, and the howling of wolves became more fierce and constant than usual. "A portent of war, a warning of punishment for sin—such were these signs, so the colonists declared—a menace of coming punishment for swearing, for not bringing up their children more strictly in religious observances, for the wearing of long hair by the men and of gay clothing by the women. The more extreme Puritans even said they were about to be "judged" for not exterminating the Quakers."

And still silently, busily, Philip and his savage forest nation were making preparations for war, wide-spread and devastating.

The colonists sent a peremptory message to the great leader to appear at a conference and give a reason for his warlike acts, of which they had heard. He sent a peremptory refusal. A second and more imperative summons was sent, and, feeling that another refusal would only confirm the suspicions against him, Philip and his train of brilliantly adorned braves marched to within four miles of Taunton, and sent a message to the English governor, requesting him to come there and confer with him. The governor refused, but sent several able colonists to assure the haughty monarch of his entirely friendly feeling, and to beg Philip to go on to Taunton. Philip held the messengers as hostages for his safe return, and marched on to Taunton with his impressive retinue.

On the outskirts of the village he again halted, and, establishing sentinels around his encampment, received the Massachusetts commissioners with grave courtesy and gave his consent to a conference in the meeting-house, provided, so he said, that half of the building might be appropriated to the exclusive use of his warriors, while his accusers should have the other half, and the commissioners were to sit alone as umpires. These haughty demands having been acceded to, the conference was opened.

Solemnly a speaker for the colonists preferred the charges against Philip, and with equal solemnity the great chief arose to make his answer. "The English," he said, "richly deserve a countercharge of depredations on our property and land—and in answer to the question of my warlike preparations, surely I have a right to protect my people against the powerful and warlike Narragansetts!"

Immediately a colonist arose with conclusive contradictory evidence, which Philip parried with the skill of a diplomat, but after a long and tedious conference, so old records tell us, Philip, standing in military erectness and with an imperious air, confessed his preparations for war, made a treaty of friendship, and allowed his seventy warriors to surrender their guns to the governor of Plymouth, to be held as long as he should distrust the sincerity of their vows. Philip also promised to send in the guns of his absent warriors before the autumn. It was agreed, too, that in case of further trouble between colonists and Indians both should submit their complaint to the arbitration of Massachusetts.

Then the council adjourned, and the long line of warriors and Puritans filed out of the little meeting-house and went their various ways.

Treaty and promise were soon alike forgotten by the Indians, who had merely made them to extricate themselves from a dilemma, and there were new and bitter complaints made against Philip by the Plymouth colonists. To vindicate himself from these he went to Boston, where much respect was paid the proud young monarch, whose athletic figure was well set off "by a coat and buckskins set thick with beads, in pleasant wild-work, and a broad belt of the same." His accoutrements were valued at twenty pounds, being decorated with beads, which are Indian money.

So cleverly did Philip confer with the Boston authorities that after hearing his story they despatched a letter to Plymouth, in which they said:

"We do not understand how Philip hath subjected himself to you. But the treatment you have given him and your proceedings toward him do not render him such a subject as that, if there be not a present answering to summons, there should presently be a proceeding to hostilities. The sword once dipped in blood may make him as independent upon you as you are upon him."

Again a council was called, this time between the four

New England colonies and the Wampanoags, and again Philip confessed himself the author of trouble, and promised to pay one hundred pounds, "in such things as he had," as an indemnity for the expense to which he had subjected the colony, and promised also to deliver "five wolves' heads" annually in additional payment for his misdemeanors. With this promise he and his braves filed out of the meeting-house and left Plymouth, to maintain a doubtful peace with the Puritans for three years, while Philip's plans were maturing.

His great confederacy was to include all the New England tribes except the remaining Pequots and the Mohegans, and in the spring of 1676 the confederated tribes were to make a simultaneous attack on all the settlements in New England, so that the colonies could not aid one another, by which great attack the extermination of the English was to be accomplished.

Philip meanwhile grew more and more aggressive in his acts, and so bold in manner that the governor sent an ambassador to demand an explanation of such hostilities. Drawing his mantle around him in haughty dignity, Philip said:

"Your governor is but a subject of King Charles of England. I shall not treat with a subject. I shall only treat with the king, my brother. When he comes, I am ready!" And on went preparations for war and acts of hostility on the part of the Indians. That the great Wampanoag leader dreaded the war, and actually shed tears in the opening act of the bloody drama, is an historical fact, and his reason for resisting the colonists lay in a stern resolve to do his duty to his people. As he nobly said:

"The English who came first to this country were but a handful of people, forlorn, poor, and distressed. My father did all in his power to serve them. Their numbers increased.

My father's councilors were alarmed. They urged him to destroy the English before they became strong enough to give law to the Indians and take away their country. My father was also the father to the English. We remained their friend. Experience shows that his councilors were right. The English disarmed my people. They tried them by their own laws and assessed damages my people could not pay. Sometimes the cattle of the English would come into the corn-fields of my people, for they did not make fences like the English. I must then be seized and confined till I sold another tract of my country for damages and costs. Thus tract after tract is gone. But a small part of the dominion of my ancestors remains. I am determined not to live until I have no country."

"This," says a chronicler of the times, "is the sad note of preparation sounded by a royal leader, that summons to their last conflict the aboriginal lords of New England."

"War was in the air now—young braves, always eager for excitement and combat, roamed about the country sharpening their knives and tomahawks on the door-sills of the colonists," and boasted in loud voices of the deeds they were about to do in the name of their mighty chief. At the same time a Christian Indian, John Sassasmon, employed by King Philip to sign his documents and write his letters, having learned of the plan for confederation and war, betrayed Philip to the English, and for the act was summarily killed. Three noted Indians, all members of Philip's council, were arrested for the murder, brought before a jury of eight Englishmen and four Indians, convicted and hung; and Philip's rage knew no bounds, not only because of Sassasmon's treachery, but because, as he asserted, "The English had nothing to do with one Indian's killing another."

He was also much afraid that he himself might be hung for implication in the murder, which had most certainly been executed at his order, but, although old records show that there was a plot to kill him, it was not carried out, and on went his preparations for war.

Bands of marauding Indians now constantly annoyed the inhabitants of every settlement and carried terror to the most courageous settlers on solitary farms or on the outskirts of villages.

On a lovely Sabbath in late June, while most of the inhabitants of the little settlement of Swansea, Massachusetts, were attending service in their small meeting-house, eight Indians invaded the quiet streets, ransacked several houses, and finally demanded a colonist's permission to grind their hatchets on his grindstone. The settler answered that, being the Lord's Day, they could not do such work. The invaders replied, "We care neither for your God nor for you, but we will grind our hatchets!" and, entering the house by force, ransacked it, then went noisily down the road until they met another settler, whom they immediately captured, and made him walk with them for quite a distance, taunting and annoying him in every way possible, finally setting him free with the parting injunction to "be a good man and not tell any lies or work on the Lord's day."

Having left him, they roamed on, shooting cattle and plundering supplies at will. Finally they demanded entrance at a cabin where the man of the house became so provoked by their acts that he seized his gun and shot one of the young Indians. Breathing vengeance on the whole white race, his comrades lifted him up and carried him away on their shoulders, and the first blood in King Philip's War had been shed.

The people of Swansea then appointed the next Thursday

for a day of fasting and prayer. On that day the village wore the stillness of a Sabbath. Wood says: "The pious people were returning with thoughtful faces from the log church. The rough streets, filled with stumps, wound past the cabins with their little clearings, and through the noon-day shadows of the primeval forest. Suddenly there came two sharp reports, two puffs of smoke, and two near-by forms lay prostrate—one of them dead. The English were dumb with horror. Two men who were despatched for a "chirurgeon" were shot dead in the road; at the same time red flames burst through the roofs of a dozen cabins.

Two settlers who had gone from their house to the well for water were shot and killed; and the savages, rushing from their hiding-place, seized the bodies, dragged them into the forest, and scalped them. A young girl hid two children left in her care under a large brass kettle, then fired at an Indian who was forcing entrance into the cabin, but, failing to kill him, beat him off by throwing a shovelful of live coals in his face so that he was found in the woods dead from his wounds.

"'Kill—burn—destroy!' were the commands of the savage monarch of Mount Hope, who was the presiding genius of the conflict, and under his direction his followers gleefully did their work of destruction. Flushed with victory, the Indians skulked everywhere, and none could venture abroad without danger of being shot."

Runners were immediately sent out from all the frontier towns to Plymouth and Boston, begging for assistance, and in three hours after a messenger arrived in Boston one hundred and twenty men were on the march to attack Philip at Mount Hope. But the great chief had been much too wary to remain in a place almost surrounded by water, and, having first sent his family to a safe retreat, had encamped with his warriors in the great Pocasset Swamp.

The little army from Boston then marched on to Swansea, where they established their headquarters at the house of a Baptist clergyman, who was eager to protect his people from the Indians. The troops immediately went on a reconnoitering expedition, and crossed a bridge near the Swansea garrison-house. Shots rang out from an ambush by the roadside, and one soldier was killed and another wounded. The remainder pursued the fleeing Indians, but they darted to cover in the swamp and disappeared.

On the eastern slope of Narragansett Bay there was a small tribe of Indians called the Soykonates, whose chief, a woman named Awashonks, was highly esteemed by all her subjects, and could command three hundred warriors in time of war. Awashonks had sold part of her lands to the colonists, among them Captain Church, who had settled on a fertile spot on the shore of the bay, and with whom Awashonks was on the most friendly terms. Because of this, and also because her force would be very feeble compared with the troops of the English or of Philip, she had remained neutral as long as possible.

But now Philip sent six chiefs to ask her alliance in his interests. Awashonks meditated, then, calling a young brave, she sent him to ask Captain Church's presence at a council, and at the same time gathered her warriors for the conference. Abbott says:

"The forest rang with their shouts, the perspiration dripped from their limbs, and they were already wrought to a pitch of intense excitement." Awashonks herself led the dance, and her graceful figure appeared to great advantage in contrast with the gigantic muscular development of her warriors. The wild festivities were at their height when

Captain Church arrived in answer to Awashonks's summons.

Immediately the dance ceased. Awashonks sat down, called her chiefs and the Wampanoags around her, and invited Captain Church to take a conspicuous seat in the midst of the group.

Then in a speech of queenly courtesy she informed the Englishman that Philip had sent his men to beg her to enter into a confederacy against the whites, and stated that the English, having raised a great army, were about to invade the territory of the Wampanoags, his people, and exterminate them.

She then called on Philip's chiefs to approach, and they filed forward and stood before the assemblage, a striking group of warriors in their barbaric war-dress, "their faces painted, their hair trimmed in the fashion of the crests of the ancient helmets, their knives and tomahawks sharp and glittering, and their guns, horns, and pouches abundantly supplied with shot and powder."

Braves and captain pleaded their cause earnestly. Awashonks, anxious to keep on good terms with the great leader of the Wampanoags, yet with a strong inclination to side with the English, finally told Captain Church that Philip's real message was that he would send his men over privately to shoot the cattle and burn the houses of the settlers who were within his territory, and so make the English fall in vengeance on her, whom they would naturally suppose to be the cause of the trouble.

Enraged at this, the captain angrily advised Awashonks to knock the warriors on the head and throw herself on the protection of the English; but the Indian queen was too discreet for any move like that, and with gracious words and smiles dismissed the Indians unharmed, then assured

Captain Church that she should look to his nation for friendship and protection.

Happy at this result of the council, he went at once to the headquarters of the Pocasset tribe, of which Wetamoo, the wife of Alexander, former chief of the Wampanoags, was a princess. Her power was equal to that of Awashonks, and she could lead three or four hundred warriors into battle, so Captain Church was eager to enlist her sympathies on his side. But the desire to avenge her husband's death still burned fiercely in Wetamoo's heart, and she dismissed the Englishman in a few imperious words and at once joined Philip's confederacy, while Awashonks, too, unmindful of her promise to Captain Church, soon united with the great chieftain's army.

The war was indeed begun—was, in fact, now raging with all the horrors of pillage and bloodshed. "The Indians in small bands went prowling over the country, and often attacked a solitary cabin in the wilderness or on the edge of a remote settlement, leaving disaster and death in their wake; or dashed into the larger towns in terrific midnight onset, slaughtering with musket and tomahawk. From far and near, throughout the vast tract occupied by the New England colonies, volumes might be written of the ghastly tragedies enacted in those early days of the Indian war." Abbott says: "None could sleep at night without fear of an attack from the Indians before the morning. In the silence of the wilderness many a tragedy was enacted of terror, torture, and blood which would cause the ear that hears of it to tingle."

On the next day, after the English force arrived in Swansea, the defiant yells of the Indians called them out to fight. The great Philip himself was with the savages when a party of volunteers rushed furiously out in pursuit of them, killed a number, and pursued the others for over a mile toward Mount Hope. The English then pushed on and up the hill to Mount Hope. Not an Indian was found on the Neck! All that was found were eight poles in line bearing the heads of eight Englishmen—ghastly trophies of a savage victory. These the English reverently took down and buried.

The Indian corn-fields around Mount Hope were now in luxuriant growth, for Philip had over a thousand acres planted. These fields the English trampled down, and destroyed all the buildings on the Neck, leaving it a bleak and barren place—which was a heavy blow to Philip, who depended on the corn to protect his people from starvation in the coming months; and to revenge this injury the Indians scattered in every direction, carrying terror, conflagration, and misery in their wake, while Captain Church, with his troops, was marching toward the territory of Awashonks. As he looked at the hill near by it seemed to move, being completely covered by Indians, with their bright guns glittering in the sun, running in a circle with an evident intention to surround the troops.

The captain and his men retreated slowly toward the shore to prevent this, but it was in vain. With hideous cries the Indians closed around them, and the situation of the English seemed desperate. They had no means of crossing the water, and the shrieking foes were pressing nearer with fiendish yells and a storm of bullets. The ground was very stony, and with a quick impulse every man began to build a breastwork for himself, while beating back the savages as fiercely as possible.

For six hours this continued, while the Indians, in ambush behind every stump, rock, or tree they could avail themselves of, kept up an incessant firing. The colonists were almost exhausted, and their store of ammunition was very low, when a sloop was seen crossing the water.

As it neared shore the Indians fired at it so effectively that its sails and sides were riddled with bullet-holes, but with great caution the vessel was steered toward the beach, and one by one the Englishmen embarked. The last to leave shore was Captain Church, who went boldly, facing his foes and presenting his gun, while a bullet passed through his hat, cutting off a lock of his hair. Two other bullets struck the canoe as he entered it, and a fourth buried itself in a stake which stood in front of him. So surrounded, he discharged a farewell shot at the enemy, was conveyed safely on board, and with his men was taken to the English garrison which since Philip's retreat to the swamp had been established at Mount Hope.

Every move in Philip's game of war showed his masterly ability to conduct a campaign according to the rules of successful warfare, and to capture him would practically end the war, the colonists knew. Large rewards were offered for his head, and he was obliged to look to it that in some unconscious moment he might not be surprised and killed.

On the 18th of July several hundred men from Taunton and Plymouth surrounded the swamp where the Indians were and attempted to come near them. Philip, on watch, saw this attempt, and his eyes gleamed with cunning as he commanded several warriors to show themselves and so lure the enemy on. Excited by the sight of the foe, the colonists pressed forward. Suddenly from the dense thicket other Indians poured a volley of shot on their pursuers, and fifteen dropped dead on the spot, while many others were wounded. Those who survived fled hastily from the swamp, "finding it ill," says Hubbard, "fighting a wild beast in his own den," and there was no more invading of the swamp.

That having failed, the English still surrounded the swamp and so cut off every possible way of escape for Philip's band, knowing that if this could be kept up long enough the Indians' provisions would give out and they would be forced to surrender. With this in view, the soldiers built a fort on the edge of the swamp and kept guard there for thirteen days. Meanwhile Philip was constructing canoes and rafts, and one dark night he and two hundred warriors floated silently across the river and with Wetamoo and her warriors fled away toward the unknown wilderness of northern Massachusetts, beyond the reach of the discomfited English! Exasperated by the escape of their enemy, they accepted the help of the Mohegans, and pursued and overtook the fleeing Indians near Providence, shooting thirty of them without losing a single man. But the great Philip himself had evaded them and was even then in the trackless forest wilderness of central Massachusetts, where he could at any point dash out to attack the New England frontier.

This was an added dread to the colonists, who, knowing that the Nipmuck Indians, a powerful tribe overspreading the whole interior of the state, were tributary to the Wampanoags, and, fearing that they might join King Philip's forces, speedily sent messengers to treat with them, and a conference with them was arranged to be held near Brookfield, Massachusetts, on the second day of August.

Promptly at the appointed time the English commissioners arrived at the great elm under which the conference was to take place. Not an Indian was on hand!

With no thought of treachery, however, the Englishmen marched on some miles farther to a spot where they felt sure the Indians would be found. Single file through a narrow path they tramped, with mud and brush under foot, and the eternal silence of the forest around them; and as they marched, three hundred Indians rose up from ambush on either side of the pass and showered a rain of bullets on them, yelling like fiends and brandishing bloody weapons.

Eight of the troop dropped dead, and many others were wounded; then the savages rushed into Brookfield, a little settlement of eighty families, and with terrified cries of "Indians! Indians!" the inhabitants had just time to flee to the garrison-house for protection when the savages were on them.

Peering from windows and loopholes of their place of refuge, the settlers watched the flare of torches, saw sudden flames rise from their cabins and reduce them in a few moments to smoldering piles of ashes.

Then the Indians surrounded the garrison and tried to burn it, too, but, being unsuccessful, kept up a series of attacks for two days, while the horrified and now nearly exhausted prisoners noted every move of the enemy with agony, for their stores of food and ammunition were low, and how could they be replenished? At last the Indians "filled a cart with hemp, flax, and the boughs of firs and pines, and fastened to the tongue a succession of long poles; then, setting the whole pile on fire, as it rolled up volumes of flame and smoke, pushed it against the log house, whose walls were as dry as dust." With bated breath and clenched hands the colonists sent up a last prayer for deliverance—and lo, it was at hand! Major Willard, of Boston, with forty dragoons, at that critical moment arrived and charged on the Indians, scattering them to right and left; then entered the garrison. His men rolled the burning cart away from the building, a providential shower came up and helped to extinguish the flames, and the savages, howling with rage at having been balked when so near victory, retired, having lost during the siege about eighty warriors, while only one white man had been killed.

The great Philip arrived at Brookfield on the day following, and, hearing of the defeat of his forces, commanded a march to the valley of the Connecticut, his presence infusing fresh courage in the ranks of his warriors.

"Passing slowly northward along the banks of the river, the Indians made almost simultaneous attacks on the little towns of Hatfield, Deerfield, Northfield, and Springfield, while Northampton, Worcester, and Hadley became battlefields indeed, and in all of the conflicts the Indians were decidedly victors. The rush on Deerfield, which was made on the 1st of September, laid the whole town in ashes, though, as in Brookfield, the inhabitants had time to take refuge in the garrison-house, and only one settler was killed."

Leaving the usual desolation and misery in their wake, the savages then passed on up the river to Northfield, where they destroyed much property and shot ten inhabitants, the remainder being safe in the garrison. This was not known at Hadley, and the next day a detachment of infantry under Captain Beers was sent from that settlement with a convoy of provisions to reinforce the Northfield garrison.

When the troops had nearly reached Northfield several hundred Indians in ambush jumped out and surrounded the soldiers, who, though they fought bravely, were all but a few killed, while the exulting Indians, under the command of Philip himself, took possession of all their luggage and provisions, and amused themselves by cutting off the heads of their victims, which they fixed on the tops of tall poles as trophies. The few survivors then straggled on to Northfield to tell their sad tale to the disheartened garrison, now almost destitute of powder and food. But help was at hand, for Major Treat was approaching with a force of one hundred and sixty Mohegans from Connecticut, and soon arrived, having had no worse experience than the terrible sight of the Hadley victims on the spot where the Indian trophies were displayed.

As soon as he reached Northfield, Major Treat decided that the Indians were too numerous in that region for him to take any more chances against them, and broke up the garrison so hastily that he did not even stop to destroy property, as was customary, marching on as fast as possible.

Meanwhile in the Deerfield garrison-house there were three thousand bushels of corn, and on the 18th of September Captain Lothrop, with one hundred men, had been despatched to bring this corn to Hadley. The wagons were loaded, the trip was begun in safety, and not an Indian was seen as the party journeyed on. "All went well," Wood says, "until they reached the banks of a beautiful little stream. It was a bright autumn day. Grape-vines festooned the gigantic forest trees . . . and purple clusters hung in profusion among the boughs. Captain Lothrop allowed his men to throw their guns into the carts and to stroll about gathering grapes."

Hark! a crackling in the underbrush—stealthy footsteps. Yelling exultantly, Indians rushed out from every side of the forest and poured a deadly fire of bullets on the soldiers, who were taken so by surprise that they could only imitate the Indian method of fighting, each one from behind a tree. But they were overpowered and surrounded. "Some in their terror climbed into the branches of trees, hoping to be overlooked, but the savages, glancing up, taunted them, brought them down and killed them, and of all that gallant force only eight escaped to tell of the tragedy; and since that day the little stream running through the south end of Deerfield meadow, on whose banks the tragedy occurred, has been known as Bloody Brook, from the color of its waters, said to have run red from the date of the fearful slaughter."

Captain Mosely had been left in the garrison-house at Deerfield with seventy men. Being only five miles beyond Bloody Brook, he heard the firing and instantly went out to the relief of the troops, but he was too late. Finding the scene of bloody desolation, he fell upon the Indians and fought fiercely there for six hours, with the fortunate reinforcement of Major Treat and his Mohegans. Together the two captains fought so vigorously that the Indians at last fled, leaving ninety-six of their number dead, to the great dismay of Philip, whose forces were now dwindling.

Mosely and Treat encamped in an open space for the night, and attended to the burial of the dead, placing them in two pits—the colonists in one and the Indians in the other. A slab was placed over the mound covering this, and a monument marks the spot where the battle of Bloody Brook was fought.

A brilliant idea now dawned on the minds of the wearied and disheartened colonists. If union is strength, they would make the test of it to put a stop to this war of Philip's. Commissioners were appointed from the different colonies to form a confederation and act in concert, with not less than a thousand troops. The number was quickly raised, and the whole command was given to Colonel Josiah Winslow, of Plymouth.

While the colonists were thus gathering their forces together, the Narragansetts annulled their treaty with them, and their chief, Canonchet, the most remarkable Indian taking part in the war except Philip, helped him to erect a strong fortification in the large swamp where the Indians were intrenched. The fort was built on high ground near the middle of the swamp, surrounded by an impenetrable hedge and imposing palisades and breastworks. Here were built, too, five hundred log houses, almost bullet-proof. The only entrance to the fortification was by a bridge over deep water, the bridge made of the trunk of a large tree so narrow that persons crossing it were obliged to walk single file. As this bridge was also flanked by a blockhouse, the whole plan was an admirable example of Philip's genius.

Soon three thousand warriors under the united command of Philip and Canonchet were gathered at this place, where, on the 19th of December, they were surprised by the colonists, who had been guided to the bridge by a treacherous Indian.

Down the narrow bridge, one by one, rushed the English, but were instantly shot down by Philip's warriors. In a few moments six captains and a large number of men were dead or dying in the ditch, while a few who had succeeded in crossing the tree were killed by the bullets of the savages hiding behind the breastworks.

At last Captain Church, who was in command of the English, seeing a point at the rear of the fort where the guard was not strong, forced an entrance. In a moment he was supported by hundreds more of his men, and as soon as they were within the enclosure the mortal combat commenced—the combat which was the great struggle of New England; the colonists fighting for the homes they had reared in blood and hardship on the shores of the new land; the three thousand Indians, inspired by intense patriotism, hatred of the English, and a burning sense of injustice done them, fighting for equality of law and freedom.

For three hours the conflict raged, with tremendous loss of life on both sides. "At last the Indians' ammunition ran low, and above the din of war was heard Captain Church's shout, 'Fire the wigwams!' The order was obeyed, and to the tumult of battle was added the wailing of women and children and the roar of flames. Both sides fought like savages, giving no quarter and asking none. Night came on, and with it a blinding snow-storm, and the Indians retreated to the smoky depths of the swamp, many of them to perish with the cold."

The English were left in possession of the fort, but theirs was a dearly bought victory. "Since daybreak they had marched sixteen miles and fought this terrible battle without food or rest. Even now, the victory won, they could not stop to rest, but hastily collected their dead and wounded, and, placing them on rough litters, wearily tramped away into the forest on the return march." As they stumbled on, often plowing their way through deep snow, many a brave man died of exhaustion, and all realized the horror of a victory which had been won at such a price.

The Indians who escaped, led by the mighty and still undaunted Philip, now went into retreat, and made no more attacks on persons or settlements until spring. Then Philip, realizing the greatness of his undertaking, called together his warriors, and with hot words lashed them into a fresh fury of rebellion, which resulted in attacks on the settlements of Lancaster, Medfield, Groton, and Marlboro, which were all left in ashes. Weymouth, near Boston, shared the same fate, and by evidences of murder and conquest on every side it would have seemed that the savage party was to be the triumphant one. But the great commander Philip was a man of vision who knew only too well the mental superiority of the white men over that of his warriors—knew, in fact, that the end of his war was near.

In April the mighty Canonchet, a brave as rare in brain as he was in body, was captured. The English offered to spare his life if he would bring about a treaty of peace, but Canonchet turned a glance of withering scorn on them and refused to listen to the suggestion. When they asked him to surrender some of Philip's men who were with him formerly, he replied, "Not a Wampanoag nor the paring of a Wampanoag's nail shall be delivered up!" When told that he must die, he made this memorable remark, "I like it well; I shall die before my heart is soft or I have said anything unworthy of myself."

"Because of his refusal to surrender his friends to certain death or to slavery, his father was murdered, his warriors killed by the hundred, and his wife and children burned in their homes; yet he said no word of reproach, simply folded his arms, and, with head erect and eye that never quailed, received the fatal bullets in his heart." In the history of his race there is no more heroic soul than this loyal friend of King Philip, and his death was a cruel blow to the Wampanoag chief, not only because of the strong personal bond between them, but because he was an ally whose place could never be filled.

The Wampanoags were growing discontented. Since their stores of corn had been destroyed by the English they had been living mainly on meat, which disagreed with many of them. Philip had promised them easy victories, they said, and much plunder, and as yet there had been only hardships, suffering, and defeat. They were sick at heart of their continued failure to wipe the English off the earth.

Captain Church made offers of peace to all who had wit enough to see how hopeless the cause of the Indian was; and several bands broke their alliance with Philip's party, to take up arms on the English side, among them Queen Awashonks and her tribe, who fought for the remainder of the war under the command of the captain to whom she had always been friendly.

When this news was brought to Philip he made no sign of regret, not a fleeting expression of chagrin crossed his inscrutable face, but it is said he never smiled again. He knew now that his doom was sealed, even though Wetamoo and her remaining warriors were still loyal to him.

Throughout New England there were traitorous Indians to be found who were only too willing to sell information in regard to the plans of their chief, and one of these now traveled to Taunton and offered to conduct the English to the river where Wetamoo was in hiding.

Arming themselves, twenty men followed their guide to a place near Swansea, where they surprised and captured every one but the queen herself. "Too proud to be taken, when capture meant slavery, the heroic princess threw off her clothing and, seizing a broken piece of wood, plunged into the stream; but, weakened by famine and exhaustion, she sank, and soon after her body was washed ashore. The English immediately cut off her head and set it upon a pole in a street in Taunton—an act worthy of the worst barbarian of the woods; and when Wetamoo's subjects, who were taken captive to Taunton, saw the indignity which had been offered to their dead sovereign they shrieked with horror and grief."

Philip's situation as presiding genius of the war was now desperate. From place to place he fled, only to be followed by Captain Church and his men, who attacked him from every hiding-place and covert, and on the first of August met the mighty monarch's forces and killed or captured one hundred and thirty of them. Philip himself fled so hastily that his wampum-belt, covered with beads and silver, the badge of his royal office, fell into the hands of the

English, who also captured his wife and only son, young Pometacom, sold them into slavery, and shipped them both to the West Indies.

Deserted by most of his warriors, "with the Connecticut Indians now his bitter foes and the Mohawks on the Hudson thirsting for his blood, the condition of the heroic and unfortunate monarch of the Wampanoags was deplorable, for he was now a fugitive and almost alone in the support of the cause for which he had risked so much, although a few of the more noble Indians still adhered loyally to him. His domain, which had once spread over wide leagues of forest and mountain, was now contracted to the dark and dismal swamp where, like a hunted animal, he sought refuge from his pursuers."

But still the indomitable leader would not think of yielding. He determined to fight until he should fall by the hand of the enemy, and when a warrior urged him to surrender, with ineffable scorn Philip gazed at him in silence and condemned him to death. The brother of this Indian, enraged at the chief's act, at once went to the English and offered to guide them to Philip's retreat, which offer was eagerly accepted.

Abbott says: "It was now evening. Philip was upon a little spot of upland in the midst of a miry swamp south of Mount Hope. Half of the night was spent in crossing the water in canoes. At midnight Captain Church called all his company together and gave minute directions. . . . They surrounded the swamp. With the earliest light of the morning they were ordered to creep cautiously on their hands and knees until they came in sight of their foes. As soon as any one discovered Philip or any of his men he was to fire, and immediately all were to rise and join the pursuit. To make sure of his victim, Captain Church also formed a second circle around the swamp, placing an Englishman and an Indian behind trees, rocks, and stumps, so that none could pass between them. He also stationed small parties in ambuscade, and awaited results."

The night before this it is said that Philip had dreamed of falling into the hands of the English, and, waking, had told the dream to his men, advising them to flee before it should come true. When they urged that he, too, attempt to escape, he shrugged his shoulders and shook his head. He would not flee now, but he intended to keep awake at night that he might not be taken by surprise; yet, exhausted by days and nights of the hardest kind of fighting and fleeing, despite his resolve, he slept soundly, with a few faithful warriors dozing by his side.

"Silently, stealthily, while he slept, the English crept cautiously within musket-shot of the great warrior, and his men discharged a volley of bullets on them, then rushed into the encampment. Philip, roused by the whistling of bullets and the shouts of the enemy, leaped from his bed of leaves and like a hunted animal jumped from hummock to hummock in the swamp, but in his flight he ran directly in front of an Englishman and the Indian who had betrayed him, standing behind a large tree with their guns cocked and primed. Bewildered, and fleeing for his life, Philip came near the Englishman, who took deliberate aim at him and sprung his lock. The heavy dew had so moistened the powder that his gun missed fire, but the Indian then took aim at the chief to whom he had owed allegiance only a short time before. A sharp report rang through the still forest. The courageous chieftain swayed, quivered, then fell in the mud and water of the swamp. The great Philip was dead."

Eagerly the Indian traitor rushed with the news to Cap-

THE DEATH OF KING PHILIP

tain Church, and by a preconcerted signal Church called his men together and told them the good tidings. Philip was dead! The corpse was dragged out of the swamp, as if it had been the carcass of a wild beast, to where the ground was dry, and Captain Church decreed, "Forasmuch as he has caused many an Englishman's body to lie unburied and to rot above the ground, not one of his bones shall be buried." An old Indian executioner was then ordered to cut off his head and quarter his body. One of his hands, which had been disfigured by the bursting of a pistol, was given to the Indian who shot him, as his share of the spoils, and he not only had it preserved, but went around the country getting "many a penny by exhibiting it." The head was cut off from the body and sent to Plymouth, where it was set up on a gibbet and exposed for twenty years, in the hideous custom of those barbaric times.

Such "was the fate of Philip, whose mode of making war," says Baylies, "was secret and terrible. He seemed like a demon of destruction hurling his bolt in darkness. With noiseless steps, and shrouded by the deep shade of midnight, he glided from the gloomy depths of the woods. He stole on the villages and settlements of New England like the pestilence, unseen and unheard. His dreadful agency was felt when the yells of his followers roused his victims from their slumbers, and when the flames of their blazing habitations glared upon their eyes. His pathway could be traced by the horrible desolation of its progress, by its crimson prints upon the snows and the sands, by smoke and fire, by houses in ruins, by the shrieks of women, the wailing of infants, and the groans of the wounded and the dying. Well indeed might he have been called 'the Terror of New England,' yet in no instance did he transcend the ordinary usages of Indian warfare." Though he has been painted in black colors by those who were his natural enemies, in reality he possessed one of the noblest natures ever found among his savage race, and throughout the war there were constant and conspicuous examples of his kindness to individuals.

The death of Philip was such a practical termination of the war that, on the 6th of November following, a treaty of peace was made with the English on terms which, although by many thought humiliating, were certainly preferable to allowing the horrible struggle to continue. So ended a struggle in which it is estimated that six hundred men, women, and children were killed, twelve hundred houses burned, and eight thousand cattle destroyed. For a savage monarch like King Philip pitted against a commander such as Captain Church there can be no final victory in warfare, but be it to the lasting credit of such a noble Indian as the king of New England tribes that he fought with a high ideal and a lofty purpose.

"He had fought a relentless war, but he fought for his native land, and in the tragic manner of his race—fought a losing game, even though he was, perhaps, the most illustrious savage on the North American continent."

Indomitable King of New England tribes, justly do his descendants boast their ancestry and do him honor!

JOSEPH

JOSEPH: PATRIOT OF THE NEZ PERCÉS

"OLD JOSEPH," hereditary chief of the lower Nez Percés, had many times said his say against the encroachments of the white man in Oregon. Finally, the Great Father at Washington sent word that the lower Nez Percés must go on the Lapwai reservation, there to be protected and helped by the government. Old Joseph said: "I will not. I do not need your help; we have plenty, and we are contented and happy if the white man will let us alone. The reservation is too small for so many people with all their stock. . . . Our fathers were born here. Here they lived. Here they died. Here are their graves. We will never leave them."

So firm in his refusal to leave the beautiful Wallowa Valley, which was his by inheritance, was the old chief, that, seeing the strength of his opposition, the government ceased pressing its claims for a time, and the Nez Percés enjoyed peace and freedom for a brief season.

But old Joseph was becoming daily more infirm, and one day sent for his son, Joseph, that he might speak to him of those things which were in his heart.

"My son," the old chief said, "my body is returning to my mother earth, and my spirit is going very soon to see the Great Spirit Chief. When I am gone, think of your country. You are the chief of these people. They look to you to guide them. Always remember that your father never sold his country. You must stop your ears whenever you are asked to sign a treaty selling your home. A few years more and the white men will be all around you. They have their eyes on this land. My son, never forget my dying words. This country holds your father's body. Never sell the bones of your father and your mother."

Young Joseph, telling of this later, said: "My father smiled and passed away to the spirit land. I buried him in that beautiful valley of 'Winding Waters.' I love that land more than all the rest of the world. A man who would not love his father's grave is worse than a wild animal."

With the blood of such a patriot hot in his veins, and with his vow to his father ringing in his ears, it is small wonder that young Joseph, now chief in his father's place, resisted the white man's encroachments with bitter determination from that hour; nor is it to be wondered at that the noble young warrior, with his superb physique and fine mental endowment—an endowment which, with military training, would have made him the equal of our noblest generals—should have been able to plan and conduct one of the most masterly retreats in the history of Indian warfare.

For a short time after old Joseph's death his band lived in peace and freedom, but the settlers, who were pouring into the country around the "valley of Winding Waters," stole the Indians' horses, branded and drove their cattle off, and took their land. Joseph said, pathetically, "We had no friend who would plead our cause before the law councils. It seemed that some of the white men who were in Wallowa were doing these things on purpose to get up a war. We knew we were not strong enough to fight them. I labored hard to avoid trouble and bloodshed. We gave up some of our country to the white men, thinking that then we could have peace. We were mistaken. The white men would not let us alone. We could have avenged our wrongs many times, but we did not. When the white men were few and we were strong we could have killed them all off, but the Nez Percés wished to live in peace.

"If we have not done so, we have not been to blame. If we ever owned the land, we own it still, for we never sold it. In the treaty councils the commissioners have claimed that our country had been sold to the government. Suppose a white man should come to me and say, 'Joseph, I like your horses and I want to buy them.' I say to him: 'No, my horses suit me. I will not sell them.' Then he goes to my neighbor and says to him, 'Joseph has some good horses. I want to buy them, but he refuses to sell.' My neighbor answers, 'Pay me the money, and I will sell you Joseph's horses.' The white man returns to me and says, 'Joseph, I have bought your horses, and you must let me have them.' If we sold our lands to the government, this is the way they were bought." Surely no world-famed lawyer could offer a more incisive answer to an argument than this!

He also said: "My name is In-mut-too-yah-lat-lat (Thunder-traveling-over-the-mountains). I am chief of the Wal-lam-wat-kin, band of Chute-pa-lu, or Nez Percés. I was born in eastern Oregon. . . . Our fathers gave us many good laws, which they had learned from their fathers. They told us to treat all men as they treat us; that we should never be the first to break a bargain; that it was a disgrace to tell a lie; that it was a shame for one man to take from another his life or his property without paying for it. We were taught to believe that the Great Spirit sees and hears everything, and that he never forgets; that hereafter he will give every man a spirit home according to his deserts; . . . this I believe, and all my people believe the same.

"We did not know there were other people besides the

Indian until about one hundred years ago, when some men with white faces came to the country. They brought many things with them to trade for furs and skins. They brought tobacco, which was new to us. They brought guns with flint stones on them, which frightened women and children. Our people could not talk with these white-faced men, but they used signs which all people understand. These men were Frenchmen, and they called our people 'Nez Percés,' because they wore rings in their noses for ornaments. These French trappers said a great many things to our fathers which have been planted in our hearts. Our people were divided in opinion about these men. Some thought they taught more bad than good. An Indian respects a brave man, but he despises a coward. He loves a straight tongue, but he hates a forked tongue. The trappers told us some truths, but some lies."

At the time when young Joseph became chief in his father's stead, the lower Nez Percés lived along the Snake River, and also occupied the Grande Ronde and Imnaha country, as well as the lovely "valley of Winding Waters"; their great trails extending for hundreds of miles along the river toward the Blue Ridge, with the Salmon River and its tributaries furnishing an immense territory over which they could hunt and roam. The main body of the tribe, or upper Nez Percés, occupied the Lapwai. These tribal boundaries had been fixed in the treaty made by Governor Stevens in 1855, and were so liberal that even old Joseph had accepted them without murmur. But when the government decided to crowd out the Indian at the expense of the white man, and in the new treaty of 1863, which old Joseph firmly resisted, excluded the Nez Percés from the Wallowa Valley, this made a permanent division in the tribe, for, though some of the Indians agreed to remain within the prescribed boundaries, calling themselves "treaty Indians," others persistently and absolutely refused to do so, and were called the "non-treaties."

Joseph's followers were foremost among the non-treaty bands, which also included a band that roamed over the wild country between the Snake and Salmon rivers, whose chief was Too-hul-hul-sute, a cross-grained old "Dreamer," or "*Too-at.*" Still another band was found above the mouth of the Grande Ronde; while White Bird, another non-treaty chief who often disputed with Joseph the command of the united forces of the malcontents, with his followers, roamed over the mountainous country along the Salmon River, having no permanent abode. The remaining non-treaties, under Hush-hush-cute, a young chief whose heart was "bad" toward the white man, was to the westward, on the opposite side of the reservation.

Altogether there were about seven hundred men, women, and children among the non-treaties, and of that number three hundred and twenty-five were warriors, who were disturbed and restless because of the increasing number of settlers occupying the Wallowa Valley.

Joseph himself was not inclined either to trouble the settlers or to go to war, because of treaty regulations. He simply agreed with the growling old Dreamer, who said: "No! No! No! We will go where we please. Who gave Washington rule over us?" and only asked for freedom to remain unmolested in his beloved valley.

It is evident that General Howard was at least in partial sympathy with this desire of Joseph's, for when in 1875, despite the Indian's opposition, the Wallowa Valley was formally opened to white settlers, the general said, "I think it is a great mistake to take from Joseph and his band of really peaceable Indians that valley, . . . and possibly Congress can be induced to let them have it for their own. . . ." Had this only been the general sentiment, how great an amount of property and loss of life might have been saved!

But the general was a servant of the government, being then in command of the military posts and Indian agencies in that part of the Northwest, and he was obliged to attempt to bring the non-treaties to an agreement with government desires.

So he called a council of the Nez Percés at Fort Lapwai, the most lovely valley in Idaho, and asked that every Indian present should express his opinions freely in regard to accepting the terms of the treaty which required the Nez Percés to live in the Lapwai.

The council was called for the third day of May, 1877, but when Joseph and his band arrived, Joseph begged that the conference might be postponed, as White Bird's band were coming from Salmon River country, and he wished to have them at the council. Consequently, General Howard deferred the interview until the next day, when White Bird with his band had marched into the valley with the Ashotins and Too-hul-hul-sute's followers.

The Indians then gathered and formed in long lines, their faces painted red, and a red line extending down the parting in the middle of the head. The men's hair was braided and tied with showy strings, and they wore gay blankets or mantles, feathered head-dresses, leggings of buckskin, and beaded moccasins, while the women were also gaily attired, and all were mounted on ponies as varied in color as the costumes of their riders.

Before the council, they rode around the garrison, wailing a weird war-song, then in single file they approached General Howard and solemnly shook hands. Joseph, with his glossy hair very smoothly braided and his face slightly rouged, sat on a low bench, with Ollicut, his brother, on the ground beside him, and the other Indians squatted on the grass in a semicircle around Too-hul-hul-sute, the old Dreamer, who announced in a clear voice: "The earth was created by God complete, and should not be disturbed by man. Any cultivation of the soil or any improvements in the way of schools or churches are crimes which must be resisted, and therefore white settlers must be kept away from the Indian's country."

To General Howard's explanation that the non-treaty Indians were in the minority in their opposition to the laws and customs of the white man and must abide by the agreement made by other tribes, the old man replied in such a surly manner that the general feared his influence would arouse excitement and opposition among the listening Indians, and hastily suggested a second adjournment of the meeting.

By the following Monday, he said, the Indians would have had ample time to confer together concerning the treaty. The idea met with hearty approval, and Indians and whites ended their second interview with smiling faces and cordial hand-shaking.

Monday, the day for the third conference, dawned clear and bright; and the Indians made an even more striking display than before, as their numbers had been swelled by more incoming bands, and all were showily attired and painted for the ceremonial occasion.

Too-hul-hul-sute was the speaker of the day. Rising, he faced General Howard, saying: "The Great Spirit Chief made the world as it is and as he wanted it, and he made a part of it for us to live upon. I do not see where you get authority to say that we shall not live where he placed us."

General Howard lost his temper, and said: "Shut up! I

don't want to hear any more of such talk. The law says you shall go upon the reservation to live, and I want you to do so, but you persist in disobeying the law [meaning the treaty]. If you do not move, I will take the matter into my own hand, and make you suffer for your disobedience."

Too-hul-hul-sute answered: "Who are you, that you ask us to talk, and then tell me I sha'n't talk? Are you the Great Spirit? Did you make the world? Did you make the sun? Did you make the rivers to run for us to drink? Did you make the grass to grow? Did you make all these things, that you talk to us as though we were boys? If you did, then you have the right to talk as you do."

General Howard replied, "You are an impudent fellow, and I will put you in the guard-house," and ordered a soldier to arrest him.

Too-hul-hul-sute made no resistance. He asked General Howard: "Is that your order? I don't care. I have expressed my heart to you. I have nothing to take back. I have spoken for my country. You can arrest me, but you cannot change me or make me take back what I have said."

The soldiers came forward and seized him, and took him to the guard-house. Joseph's men whispered among themselves whether they should let this thing be done; but Joseph advised them to submit, as he knew that if the Indians resisted, all the white men present, including General Howard, would be killed in a moment, and the Indians would be blamed.

Then, seeing the danger in which his people were placed, while the old Dreamer was being dragged away to the guard-house, Joseph himself rose, with noble determination written on every feature of his fine face.

"*I* am going to talk now!" he exclaimed. "I don't care

whether you arrest me or not!" Then, turning to his followers, he continued: "The arrest of Too-hul-hul-sute was wrong, but we will not resent the insult. We were invited to this council to express our hearts, and we have done so."

To such a height of magnanimity even a savage could not help responding, and there were no hostile words or acts as the council broke up, or later, while Joseph threaded his way among the throng of Indians, speaking words of courage and of peace.

The next day General Howard invited Joseph, with White Bird and Looking-glass, to go with him in search of land for the Nez Percés, should they consent to move to the reservation, and Joseph's narrative says:

"As we rode along we came to some good land that was already occupied by Indians and white people. General Howard, pointing to this land, said: 'If you will come onto the reservation, I will give you these lands and move these people off.'

"I replied, 'No. It would be wrong to disturb these people. I have no right to take their homes. I have never taken what did not belong to me. I will not now.'

"We rode all day upon the reservation, and found no good land unoccupied. I have been informed by men who do not lie that General Howard sent a letter that night, telling the soldiers at Walla Walla to go to Wallowa Valley and drive us out upon our return home.

"In council, next day, General Howard informed me in a haughty spirit that he would give my people thirty days to go back home, collect all their stock, and move onto the reservation, saying, 'If you are not here in that time, I shall consider that you want to fight, and will send my soldiers to drive you on.'

"I said: 'War can be avoided, and it ought to be avoided.

I want no war. My people have always been the friends of the white man. Why are you in such a hurry? I cannot get ready to move in thirty days. Our stock is scattered, and Snake River is very high. Let us wait until fall, then the river will be low. We want time to hunt up our stock and gather supplies for winter.'

"General Howard replied, 'If you let the time run over *one* day, the soldiers will be there to drive you onto the reservation, and all your cattle and horses outside of the reservation at that time will fall into the hands of the white men.'

"I knew I had never sold my country, and that I had no land in Lapwai; but I did not want bloodshed. I did not want my people killed. I did not want anybody killed. Some of my people had been murdered by white men, and the white murderers were never punished for it. I told General Howard about this, and again said I wanted no war. I wanted the people who lived upon the lands I was to occupy at Lapwai to have time to gather their harvest.

"I said in my heart that, rather than have war, I would give up my country. I would give up my father's grave. I would give up everything rather than have the blood of white men upon the hands of my people.

"General Howard refused to allow me more than thirty days to move my people and their stock. I am sure that he began to prepare for war at once."

On Joseph's return to Wallowa he found great excitement prevailing among his people. Soldiers were already in the Wallowa Valley!

A council was held at once, for the position of the government was now plain. Under the powerful influence of Joseph the Nez Percés decided to submit quietly at once to the government's demand, unjust though they felt it to be, in order to prevent bloodshed, but Too-hul-hul-sute, who had been released after five days' imprisonment in the guard-house, felt so outraged at having been arrested, simply because he had expressed his mind—when that was what the Indians had been asked to do—that he talked fiercely for war until he aroused several of the young braves to as frenzied a state as his own.

Seeing the advantage he had gained, Too-hul-hul-sute then declared that only bloodshed could wash out the disgrace General Howard had put upon him. This inflamed the young men greatly, although Joseph still begged for peace, and it is even said that he rode among his people with a pistol in each hand, declaring he would shoot the warrior who dared defy the soldiers when they came.

[At once the non-treaties began gathering together all the stock they could find in such a hurry, but were obliged to leave many of their horses and cattle in Wallowa—also, as the river was so high, other stock was lost in crossing—but the Indians themselves reached the other side in safety, and then held a ten days' council in the wonderfully picturesque natural fortress of the Rocky Cañon.

One young brave, whose father had been killed by a white man five years before, called on the council to back him up in avenging the deed, and there were others hot for war; but Joseph stood steadfastly for peace, and, feeling sure that his advice would be followed, he went out from the council to kill beef for his family.

There was bad news when he returned. The hot-blooded young brave, regardless of Joseph's advice, had avenged his father's death. Riding out from the council with other comrades, he had killed four white men, then, galloping up the cañon, he shouted: "Why do you sit here like women? The war has begun already!"]

Shocked and troubled, Joseph went from tepee to tepee, questioning every warrior, only to discover that the young men had been secretly buying ammunition; that Too-hul-hul-sute had been successful in organizing a war-party; that further talk of peace would be useless; and his heart was heavy at the thought, for, as he said: "I knew that we were too weak to fight the United States. We had many grievances, but I knew that war would bring more." He added, pathetically:

"I know that my young men did a great wrong, but I ask, Who was first to blame? They had been insulted a thousand times; their fathers and brothers had been killed; their mothers and wives had been disgraced; they had been driven to madness by whiskey sold to them by white men; they had been told by General Howard that all their horses and cattle which they had been unable to drive out of Wallowa were to fall into the hands of white men; and, added to all this, they were homeless and desperate.

"I would have given my own life if I could have undone the killing of white men by my people. I blame my young men, and I blame the white men. I blame General Howard for not giving my people time to get their stock away from Wallowa. I do not acknowledge that he had the right to order me to leave Wallowa at any time. I deny that either my father or myself ever sold that land. It is still our land. It may never again be our home, but my father sleeps there, and I love it as I love my mother. I left there, hoping to avoid bloodshed.

"If General Howard had given me plenty of time to gather up my stock, and treated Too-hul-hul-sute as a man should be treated, *there would have been no war*."

But the matter having been carried beyond his decision, Joseph was far too much of a soldier not to assume immediate command of his forces, and at once moved them to White Bird Cañon, where he awaited the coming of the soldiers.

After two days Colonel Perry, with one hundred soldiers, began at daybreak to descend the broad trail to the cañon, hoping to surprise the Indians. But Joseph never slept when at war, and his keen eyes discovered the horsemen at sunrise as soon as they came in sight, and his shouts rang out: "Get the white man's glass! Tell White Bird. Horses! The soldiers are here!"

Some of the warriors begged to move across the Salmon River to a position of safety. "No!" thundered Joseph. "We will fight them here!" Then a body of mounted warriors under White Bird took up their position in ambush behind a ridge on the south side of the cañon, while the others, with Joseph, crouched on the ground, across the trail, well hidden behind rocks and in hollows.

On came the soldiers, until they were within range of the Indians' shots. Then from their ambush they poured out volley after volley of bullets, while White Bird's men came from the left and fired at the same time. Thick and fast the soldiers fell, and they were commanded to fall back to the next ridge; but the Indians were at their heels as they obeyed the order, and while the officers were trying to rally their men the Indians rushed along the side of the cañon to head them off and cut off their retreat. Part of them reached the ascent and hurried out in safety, but the others surrendered, and most of them, together with their gallant commander, were killed. Across the country the fleet-footed Indians pursued the flying troops for twelve miles, until, four miles from Mount Idaho, Joseph withdrew his men, having fought and won his first battle, even though largely outnumbered by the enemy.

[In his own account of the battle Joseph says: "We numbered sixty men, and the soldiers one hundred. The fight lasted but a few minutes before the soldiers retreated. They lost thirty-three killed and had seven wounded. None of the soldiers were scalped. We do not believe in scalping nor in killing wounded men. Soldiers do not kill many Indians unless they are wounded and left on the battle-field. *Then* they kill Indians."]

This first encounter with the non-treaties proved to the troops that a stronger force was needed to subdue the savages, and reinforcements were ordered from all neighboring forts. While waiting for them, skirmishing with the Indians took place, and a detachment of soldiers, under Captain Whipple, was sent to subdue Chief Looking-glass's band before they had a chance to join the malcontents, but the red men were too quick for the soldiers, and Looking-glass and his warriors slipped away and immediately joined Joseph, after many of Captain Whipple's command had been killed and wounded in the encounter. General Howard, meanwhile, at Fort Lapwai was still impatiently awaiting reinforcements.

They finally arrived, and on the 11th of July the Indians, who, having crossed country to the Lapwai reservation, were now in a position on the Clearwater, where they had built breastworks of the most approved pattern and were waiting to give battle, again saw the general, who had an army of four hundred soldiers.

On the troops came, leaving their two supply-trains unguarded. With his keen, quick eye, Joseph, from a high vantage-point he had taken, saw this, and sent thirty warriors to attack the trains. An officer, watching Joseph's movement, despatched a messenger to hurry them into the lines, while a company of cavalry also galloped to their aid, but the Indians again were too quick for them. Capturing the smaller train, they killed two men and disabled their animals before the fire of the cavalry drove them off. The longer train, however, gained the lines uninjured, and the battle raged fiercely until night, when both parties took time to strengthen their positions, though still keeping up a desultory firing. At dawn the fierce combat began again, with no perceptible advantage on either side, until the middle of the afternoon, when General Howard's ranks were strengthened by the arrival of a fresh company of cavalry, which so encouraged the troops that they charged on the enemy's line at the left.

The Indians fought fiercely behind their breastworks for a while, but finally gave way and fled in all directions. From rock to rock through the ravines they bounded, plunging into the river, only to reappear when its swift current had borne them out of reach; but on pressed the victorious troops so close to them that the Indians' entire camp equipment fell into the enemy's hands, but for this the savages cared nothing. They, themselves, had escaped with their herds and some supplies, and before the troops could cross the Clearwater a large force of warriors confronted them, having returned to make another attack. While the troops hastily prepared to meet them the other Indians escaped, and the returning warriors, having by a clever feint accomplished this result, disappeared.

In the morning the troops still continued to pursue the fleeing Indians, but with no success, "and by night all the warriors were safely encamped in an almost impregnable position at the entrance of Lolo trail, and Joseph, though beaten in his second battle, had against heavy odds brought his forces out creditably."

Finding they were largely outnumbered by the troops,

the Indians now retreated through the mountain-pass to Bitter Root Valley, encumbered with women, children, and herds, and there found a hastily built fort held by Captain Rawn and a small force of regulars. Looking-glass, confronting the captain, said: "We will not fight the settlers if they do not fight us. We are going by you to the buffalo country. Will you let us go in peace?"

Rawn replied, "You cannot go by us."

To this the Indian answered, "We are going by you without any fighting if you will let us, but we are going by you anyhow!"

And go they did, not only in peace, but stopping at two villages on their way to trade with the whites. At one place they left a spy, who remained there until General Howard with his men had come up and passed on, then the spy hastened forward to give Joseph full details of the general's plan for the troops.

In Joseph's account of this he says:

"We understood that there was to be no more war. We intended to go peaceably to the buffalo country, and leave the question of returning to our country to be settled afterward.

"With this understanding we traveled on for four days, and, thinking that the trouble was all over, we stopped and prepared tent-poles to take with us. We started again, and at the end of two days we saw three white men passing our camp. Thinking that peace had been made, we did not molest them. We could have killed or taken them prisoners, but we did not suspect them of being spies, which they were.

"That night the soldiers surrounded our camp. About daybreak one of my men went out to look after his horses. The soldiers saw him and shot him down like a coyote. I have since learned that these soldiers were not those we had left behind. They had come upon us from another direction. The new white war-chief's name was Gibbon. He charged upon us while some of my people were still asleep. We had a hard fight, but we finally drove General Gibbon back.

"Finding that he was not able to capture us, he sent to his camp a few miles away for his big guns [cannon], but my men had captured them and all the ammunition. We damaged the big guns all we could and carried away the powder and lead. In the fight with General Gibbon we lost fifty women and children and thirty fighting-men. We remained long enough to bury our dead, then retreated as rapidly as we could toward the buffalo country. After six days General Howard came close to us, and we went out and attacked him, and captured nearly all his horses and mules (about two hundred and fifty head). We then marched on to the Yellowstone Basin."

There Joseph and his band encamped on the great Camas Prairie, west of the National Park. "He had replenished his supplies, captured two hundred and fifty good horses, and his forces were in fine condition. Scarcely a day's march behind on the vast prairie General Howard's troops were also encamped, and, although they seemed safeguarded, as Lieutenant Bacon had been despatched with a squad of men to hold Tacher's Pass—the most accessible roadway over the divide into the Park—and there were pickets and sentinels posted at intervals along the Indians' possible line of march," suddenly a troop of horsemen came in sight, on the Indian trail, riding in a column of four, regularly and without haste. On they came to the very lines of the soldiers' camp, and were supposed by the sentinel to be Bacon's men returning. He challenged them, and the answer was a deafening war-whoop! At once there was the wildest confusion among the troopers, the sound of shots, and the stampeding of horses and mules, who dashed away, frenzied with excitement, followed by the Indians yelling like demons. Joseph, by a bit of strategy, had given the soldiers a very successful surprise, and the Indians, eluding their enemies, retreated through Tacher's Pass to the beautiful National Park, capturing three white men and two women on the way, whom they treated kindly and released at the end of three days.

On the 9th of September a scout brought news to Joseph that General Sturgis was coming up from the Powder River country with over three hundred and fifty cavalry, besides some friendly Crows, and the brave young chief was between two horns of a dilemma. With General Howard and his force marching against him in one direction and this new regiment of cavalry coming from the south, could he again escape with his followers?

With quick and masterly strategy he and his warriors made a feint to move westward. This fooled Sturgis, and sent him on a wild-goose chase to guard a false trail, while Joseph and his men hastily made their way through a dense forest into a narrow, dark, and very slippery cañon, through which finally the troops cautiously followed them, only to find that Joseph's fleeter force had already escaped into the open.

General Sturgis had but one thing to do now, and he did it. With hot haste he and his men pursued the Indians across country, and all day the savages retreated, fighting desperately as they went, until at dusk the exhausted soldiers withdrew to camp at the mouth of the cañon, after a day without further results than having rounded up several hundred ponies which had been abandoned for fresh mounts by the Indians.

On the next day the pursuit was continued, but, try as

they would, and march and fight as they would, the soldiers could not diminish the distance between the Nez Percés and their own ranks, and the victorious Indians marched on to the Missouri, which they reached on the 23d of September, General Joseph having fought his fourth battle against a much larger force than his own, and held it in check, while he brought his own people out in comparative safety. As he modestly says in his own account, "This was the fourth army, each of which outnumbered our fighting force, that we had encountered within sixty days."

Having crossed the Missouri, the Nez Percés moved slowly on to the north, believing themselves secure now, in consequence of having repulsed the forces of General Howard, General Gibbon, and General Sturgis, and set up their camp within a day's march of Canada, on Snake Creek, a branch of the Milk River.

General Miles, the commandant at Fort Keogh, on the Yellowstone, at once took advantage of the one remaining chance to subdue the non-treaties. He immediately started north to intercept Joseph; and Joseph's narrative says:

"We had no knowledge of General Miles's army until a short time before he made a charge upon us, cutting our camp in two and capturing nearly all of our horses. About seventy men, myself among them, were cut off. My little daughter, twelve years of age, was with me. I gave her a rope, and told her to catch a horse and join the others who were cut off from the camp. I have not seen her since, but I have learned that she is alive and well.

"I thought of my wife and children, who were now surrounded by soldiers, and I resolved to go to them or die. With a prayer in my mouth to the Great Spirit Chief who rules above, I dashed unarmed through the line of soldiers. It seemed to me that there were guns on every side, before and behind me. My clothes were cut to pieces and my horse was wounded, but I was not hurt. As I reached the door of my lodge my wife handed me my rifle, saying: 'Here's your gun. Fight!'

"The soldiers kept up a continuous fire. Six of my men were killed in one spot near me. Ten or twelve soldiers charged into our camp and got possession of two lodges, killing three Nez Percés and losing three of their men, who fell inside our lines. I called my men to drive them back. We fought at close range, not more than twenty steps apart, and drove the soldiers back upon their main line, leaving their dead in our hands. We secured their arms and ammunition. We lost, the first day and night, eighteen men and three women. General Miles lost twenty-six killed and forty wounded. The following day General Miles sent a messenger into my camp under protection of a white flag. I sent my friend Yellow Bull to meet him.

"Yellow Bull understood the messenger to say that General Miles wished me to consider the situation; that he did not want to kill my people unnecessarily. Yellow Bull understood this to be a demand for me to surrender and save blood. Upon reporting this message to me Yellow Bull said he wondered whether General Miles was in earnest. I sent him back with my answer, that I had not made up my mind, but would think about it and send word soon. A little later he sent some Cheyenne scouts with another message. I went out to meet them. They said they believed that General Miles was sincere and really wanted peace. I walked on to General Miles's tent. He met me, and we shook hands. He said, 'Come, let us sit down by the fire and talk this matter over.' I remained with him all night; next morning Yellow Bull came over to see if I was alive and why I did not return.

"General Miles would not let me leave the tent to see my friend alone.

"Yellow Bull said to me: 'They have got you in their power, and I am afraid they will never let you go again. I have an officer in our camp, and I will hold him until they let you go free.'

"I said: 'I do not know what they mean to do with me, but if they kill me you must not kill the officer. It will do no good to avenge my death by killing him.'

"Yellow Bull returned to my camp. I did not make any agreement that day with General Miles. The battle was renewed while I was with him. I was very anxious about my people. I knew that we were near Sitting Bull's camp in King George's land, and I thought maybe the Nez Percés who had escaped would return with assistance. No great damage was done to either party during the night.

"On the following morning I returned to my camp by agreement, meeting the officer who had been held a prisoner in my camp at the flag of truce. My people were divided about surrendering. We could have escaped from Bear Paw Mountain if we had left our wounded, old women, and children behind. We were unwilling to do this. We had never heard of a wounded Indian recovering while in the hands of white men.

"On the evening of the fourth day General Howard came in with a small escort, together with my friend Chapman. We could now talk understandingly. General Miles said to me in plain words, 'If you will come out and give up your arms, I will spare your lives and send you to the reservation.' I do not know what passed between General Miles and General Howard.

"I could not bear to see my wounded men and women suffer any longer; we had lost enough already. General Miles had promised that we might return to our own country with what stock we had left. I thought we could start again. I believed General Miles, *or I never would have surrendered.* I have heard that he has been censured for making the promise to return us to Lapwai. He could not have made any other terms with me at that time. I would have held him in check until my friends came to my assistance, and then neither of the generals nor their soldiers would have ever left Bear Paw Mountain alive.

"On the fifth day I went to General Miles and gave up my gun, and said, 'From where the sun now stands I will fight no more.' My people needed rest—we wanted peace."

The terms of this surrender were shamefully violated. Joseph and his band were taken first to Fort Leavenworth and then to the Indian Territory. At Leavenworth they were placed in the river-bottom, where they had no water to drink but that from the muddy river.

"Many of my people sickened and died, and we buried them in this strange land," says Joseph. "I cannot tell how much my heart suffered for my people while at Leavenworth. The Great Spirit Chief who rules above seemed to be looking some other way and did not see what was being done to my people."

Then, with a magnanimous justice of which few white men would have been capable under the circumstances, Joseph added: "I believe General Miles would have kept his word if he could have done so. I do not blame him for what we have suffered since the surrender. I do not know who is to blame. We gave up all our horses, over eleven hundred, and all our saddles, over one hundred, and we have not heard from them since. *Somebody has got our horses!*"

This simple statement of Joseph's is, as Helen Hunt Jackson has said, "a very Iliad of tragedy; of dignified and hopeless sorrow," and it stands supported by the official records of the Indian Bureau.

Chief Joseph's trust in the integrity of General Miles was not misplaced. Seven years after the brave chief's surrender; he and the remainder of his band were returned to the neighborhood of their old home, which in some degree atoned for the wrong done one of the noblest Indian patriots who ever attempted to mete out justice alike to his own race and to the white men, at whose hands he suffered such cruel wrongs. Listen to a bit of Joseph's clear-cut philosophy, as he put it down in writing some years ago:

> If the white man wants to live in peace with the Indian, he can live in peace. There need be no trouble. Treat all men alike. Give them all the same law. Give them all an even chance to live and grow. All men were made by the same Great Spirit Chief. They are all brothers. The earth is the mother of all people, and all people should have equal rights upon it. You might as well expect the rivers to run backward as that any man who was born a free man should be contented when penned up and denied liberty to go where he pleases. If you tie a horse to a stake, do you expect he will grow fat? If you pen an Indian up on a small spot of earth and compel him to stay there he will not be contented, nor will he grow and prosper. I have asked some of the great white chiefs where they get their authority to say to the Indian he shall stay in one place, while he sees white men going where they please. They cannot tell me.
>
> When I think of our condition my heart is heavy. I see men of my race treated as outlaws and driven from country to country or shot down like animals.
>
> I know that my race must change. We cannot hold our own with the white men as we are. We can only ask an even chance to live as other men live. We ask to be recognized as men. We ask that the same law shall work alike on all men. If the Indian breaks the law, punish him by the law. If the white man breaks the law, punish him also.

Let me be a free man—free to travel, free to stop, free to work, free to trade where I choose, free to choose my own teachers, free to follow the religion of my fathers, free to think and talk and act for myself—and I will obey every law or submit to the penalty.

Whenever the white man treats the Indian as they treat each other, then we will have no more wars. We shall all be alike—brothers of one father and one mother, with one sky above us and one country around us, and one government for all. Then the Great Spirit Chief who rules above will smile upon this land, and send rain to wash out the bloody spots made by brothers' hands from the face of the earth. For this time the Indian race are waiting and praying. I hope that no more groans of wounded men and women will ever go to the ear of the Great Spirit Chief above, and that all people may be one people.

In-mut-too-yah-lat-lat has spoken for his people.

YOUNG JOSEPH.

SITTING BULL

SITTING BULL: MEDICINE-MAN OF THE SIOUX

RIDING slowly along a rough forest trail claimed by the Sioux, came two Crow Indians, mounted on ponies, and a woman with her papoose strapped to her back.

"Woo! Woo! Hay-ay!" Down the trail dashed another pony ridden by a young Sioux whooping and brandishing a tomahawk, while behind him galloped more Indians, who all fell upon the trespassing Crows, killed them, and dashed away, the young Sioux in proud triumph, for he had counted his first "coup," or victory, over the body of a dead enemy.

The boy was Jumping Badger, the fourteen-year-old son of Sitting Bull, a sub-chief, and when only ten years old had won the applause of his tribe by killing a buffalo, of which there were then vast herds in northern Dakota.

Now, four years later, he had counted his first coup, and Sitting Bull had a great feast spread in the boy's honor, to which he invited warriors from near and far. Besides dancing and feasting and recounting their scalp-taking and coups around the big council-fire, without which no Indian festivity is complete, each guest was given a horse in celebration of the event, and the host announced that Jumping Badger had won the right to be known henceforth by his father's name, and Sitting Bull the boy was called from that moment to the end of his eventful career.

Strong and sturdy the young Indian grew to be, until he stood almost six feet tall, as straight as a pine tree, with a finely shaped head, large nose, deep-set, keen, brown eyes—a color rare among Indians—and a broad forehead from which his heavy hair was parted and hung in two long braids.

Such was Sitting Bull, the young warrior, who possessed so much magnetism that he often won a follower simply by a glance, and of his power over men he was fully conscious.

In those days of his young manhood Sitting Bull decided to write down the happenings of his early career in the picture writing of his people. In some way he secured an old roll-call of the Thirty-first Cavalry, who were stationed at a near-by post, and on the blank pages of the book he drew sketches in brown and black inks, adding a touch of color for blankets and head-dresses, and in the corner of each sketch he drew a buffalo on its haunches. This was Sitting Bull's "totem," or symbol, and showed that the pictures were a true record of his own deeds as a warrior, killing and scalping his enemies, raiding a village with his followers, or driving a herd of stolen cattle across the plains, as well as a proof that in those days he took an active part in warfare.

But he was primarily a leader, born to command rather than to fight. Having discovered this, he "made his medicine" with prayer and fasting, after the manner of every Indian youth, then adopted all the mysterious rites and customs of a "medicine-man," and frequently at the time of a combat retired to the Medicine Lodge, communing, so he said, with the Great Spirit, from whom he received supernatural directions for the guidance of his followers. Coming out from the lodge, he would ask for news of the battle in an impassioned voice; then, with face upturned as if in invocation to the Great Spirit, he would give orders to his followers, and prophesy the outcome of the combat to an awed, responsive band of believers, who, wrapping their

SITTING BULL: MEDICINE-MAN OF THE SIOUX

blankets around them, would go silently away to do his bidding, while their leader as silently returned to the lodge to receive further communications from the Great Spirit.

So accurately did he forecast events, and so wisely did he advise the childlike savages of his band, that he soon drew around him a formidable array of chiefs, among them the great warrior Gall, the orator Running Antelope, and the fierce hostiles Crazy Horse and Rain-in-the-Face, with a score of others, who, with their leader, encamped where, as wards of the government, they could draw supplies from a quarter-circle of agencies surrounding them. Their camp was in the midst of the "bad lands" of Dakota, or great chasms of clay baked and cracked into deep fissures by the intense droughts of that climate, making the country practically impassable; and, so intrenched, they were able to defy the government. Because of the location which they had taken, and of Sitting Bull's ability as a leader, the government, in 1868, decided that he and his followers would be safer to have as friends than foes, and made a treaty which declared "the country of the North Platte and the Big Horn Mountains, which included the Black Hills, were unceded Indian territory, upon which no white man should settle, or which he should not even travel through without consent of the Indians."

This pacified the hostiles, and for seven years they galloped over the vast] plains hunting buffalo and other game at will, and fished and foraged freely in that vast region of which for so long they had been unmolested owners.

Then gold was discovered in the Black Hills, and "Away with treaty rights!" cried the great tide of miners and settlers who poured into Montana and Dakota, their peremptory demand being "Remove the Indians to Indian Territory!"

But Sitting Bull and his followers were determined. Around the great council-fire they discussed the situation and made their decision. Liberty was theirs, and theirs were the Black Hills by grant of the Great Father at Washington. Not a foot of land would they yield because of the treachery of the pale-faces!

But still the whites came crowding into the Black Hills region, and the government officials, who wished to keep peace with both Indians and white men, begged Sitting Bull and his chiefs to go peacefully onto a reservation where their rights and interests would be maintained. Several sub-chiefs, among them Spotted Tail and Red Cloud, were easily won over, but Sitting Bull, after listening to the arguments of the white men in grim, inscrutable silence, threw back his head until the muscles of his throat stood out like great ropes, and said with haughty defiance, "This is what we say to you. We will kill any white man who is found in our country without having asked our permission—as it is said in the treaty you are trying to break."

From that moment there was no end to hostilities between the settlers and the Sioux, who burned cabins, stole cattle and horses, and seized provisions for their own use.

Then two lieutenants of United States troops, returning from a survey of the Yellowstone Valley, were shot and scalped by the great war-chief Gall, and several months later, when a similar expedition again met the hostiles, a veterinary surgeon and a sutler of the company were murdered while riding unarmed and detached from the main body of soldiers, being entirely unsuspicious of any danger.

Their murderer escaped without being identified, and was at large for eighteen months, when Rain-in-the-Face, a remarkable young Sioux, was taking part in the Sun Dance, in which every young warrior is given a chance to prove his courage and endurance.

"Suspended in the air by a rawhide rope passed through slits cut in his body, the victim hangs until the flesh tears and he falls to the ground. If he faints or cries out, he is ever after called a squaw and treated as one. Rain-in-the-Face was lucky, for his tendons gave away easily and he was released after such a short suspension that Sitting Bull, watching with grim eagerness, declared the test was not severe enough. Without wincing, the young warrior defied him to do his worst, declaring that nothing could wring a moan from his lips.

"Deep slits were then cut in his back, over the kidneys, and a rope was passed through them, while for two days the young Indian swung," taunting his torturers, singing war-songs, and boasting of his deeds—among them the murder of the two men belonging to the last Yellowstone expedition. At last, Sitting Bull, satisfied that Rain-in-the-Face had proved his courage, ordered buffalo-skulls to be tied to his legs, and the added weight, with some vigorous kicking, enabled the Indian stoic to break free, after one of the most marvelous exhibitions of endurance ever seen, even among the Sioux, where that quality was not uncommon.

Rain-in-the-Face had passed muster as a warrior, but a scout who had witnessed the test and heard his boasts of murder while hanging, carried the news to General Custer, and he immediately sent a squad of soldiers, under the command of his brother, Captain Tom Custer, to arrest Rain-in-the-Face at Standing Rock Agency, where he was then drawing supplies. The self-confessed murderer was then brought before General Custer, confined in the guard-house, and condemned to die. But this was too tame an ending to his career to suit such a warrior as Rain-in-the-

Face, and he escaped, fled to the hostile camp, and sent back word to General Custer that he had joined Sitting Bull, and was awaiting his time for revenge, when, so he said, he should cut Tom Custer's heart out and eat it!

So matters stood between Sitting Bull's band and the government in 1876, when it was decided to attempt one more campaign against them, and General Terry, General Crook, and General Custer were sent out in the early spring to locate the hostile camp.

At that time of the year Sitting Bull's followers had just broken up winter camp on the bad lands, and together with a large number of Uncpapas, Cheyennes, and other tribes were moving toward the Big Horn region, because game was abundant there, and they would be far enough away from the troops to hunt in peace.

Without any idea of the campaign which was planned against them, or of concerted action, except a common desire to keep together until they should have had a promised Sun Dance, the tribes encamped together on the Rosebud River were for the moment guiltless of hostile action, when suddenly at midnight heralds on horseback awakened heavy sleepers by galloping around the great village of tepees, crying out, "Soldiers are coming!" Forty young braves had seen their trail, had surrounded General Crook and given him a running battle, but his force was surely coming—coming!

Immediately a great council of war was held, and there were prolonged and persistent calls for the prophet, the leader, the great medicine-man, Sitting Bull, to give advice.

Rain-in-the-Face, telling of the battle afterward, said:

"Sitting Bull had made big medicine way off on a hill. He came in with it. He made a big speech and said that Waukontonka [the Great Spirit] had come to him riding on an eagle. Waukontonka had told him that the long swords were coming, but the Indians would wipe them off the face of the earth. His speech made our hearts glad. Next day our runners came in and told us the long swords were coming. Sitting Bull had the squaw put up empty death lodges along the bend of the river to fool their scouts when they came and looked over the bluffs. The brush and bend hid our lodges. Then Sitting Bull went away to make more medicine, and *didn't come back till the fight was over.*" Wily Sitting Bull!

On came General Crook with his forces, only to be repulsed by the band of warriors headed by Gall, Rain-in-the-Face, Crazy Horse, Lone Bull, and other equally powerful fighters, who after beating back the white soldiers kept a close watch on their movements until sure that they had retreated so far that the Indians thought it safe to raise camp and cross the divide to the Little Big Horn. Reaching there, they lingered for a few days, enjoying the fine hunting and the wide open spaces so well adapted to celebrating their summer dances, and little did they dream that even then two other generals, Terry and Custer, were following in the wake of Crook, whom they had driven back.

Several days passed, and at noon, on the 25th of June, there were hundreds of young braves and boys on the flats playing ball and horse-racing, all of them armed, as young Indians of the plains are apt to be. Other Indians were eating their midday meal when from the south end of the camp rang out a cry:

"Woo! Woo! Hay-ay! Hay-ay! Warriors to your saddles! The white soldiers are upon us!"

On a swift pony the crier dashed through the village of tepees amid a tumult of confusion. Chiefs shouted to their bands to fight to the last moment—some cried out to let the old men and women move the children out of the path of the bullets, others advised to remain still, and already balls were whistling through the Uncpapa camp. Like hail they came from the soldiers of Major Reno's command, who had dismounted and were shooting, while already surrounded by a great crowd of Indian warriors awaiting a signal to charge on the soldiers.

Lone Bull gave the war-whoop; there was a dash made for the white men with such force that after a hot pursuit and some desperate fighting the entire body of Major Reno's command was repulsed and hemmed in by less than five hundred Indians.

Just as the charge was made on Reno's men, at the north end of the encampment, General Custer and his men were discovered approaching about two miles and a half to the south.

"Woo! Woo! Here they come!" the shout went up, as Custer and his formidable column came over the slope of the river-bank, but look—look! He is trying to ford the river at the wrong spot. Crazy Horse sees his advantage, is galloping like the wind to the right ford half a mile down-stream. Custer is still attempting to cross above—some of his men have dismounted, are examining the river-banks, have discovered their mistake, in despair are firing into the enemy's camp, but it is too late; Crazy Horse and his followers have already crossed the river, and behind them are dashing Little Horse and White Bull with the other Cheyennes, and down to the ford the Brulés and the Minneconwojus are coming to join them at breakneck speed.

Across the river and along the edge of the ravine they dashed, going east from the crossing until it passed the ridge, while Iron Star and Low Dog turned to the south immediately after crossing the river. Firing from the camp still kept up, and as the Indians came near Custer's force they opened fire on the soldiers, and forced them back toward the ridge half a mile in from the river-bank.

Again Custer saw danger too late to remedy it. One company having reached the summit of the ridge only to be forced behind the brow of the hill by the Indians, the soldiers then took up three separate positions along the ridge, but were already hemmed in by their foes. The gun-shots and deafening war-whoops so frightened the horses that many of the soldiers dismounted, and, lying on the ground, shot wildly among the whirling masses of Indians.

There was a signal for a general onslaught of the Indians, a wild charge of Crazy Horse with the Oglallas, and White Horse and White Bull with the Cheyennes. A daring soldier on a swift horse started for the river, but was brought down. Another signal for a charge—an attack from all sides. Yells of "Woo! Woo! Hay-ay! Hay-ay!" as the entire body of Indians, now armed with clubs and bows and arrows, charged again, and with the fiercest kind of fighting wiped out Custer and that gallant force with which he had gone out to quell the hostile band.

The brave general had made his last raid—had been defeated, not because he had encountered a greater number of Indians than he had expected, but because he had under-estimated their ability as warriors.

Having wiped out Custer's command, the Indians immediately surrounded Major Reno's force, and soon occupied every available spot around him, so that his escape was impossible, and kept him thus hemmed in for fourteen hours, when a scout brought news that a large boat and many soldiers were coming up the Big Horn River. A hurried council was held, camp was hastily raised, Major Reno released, and the victorious tribes hurriedly broke up into smaller parties and scattered in different directions, for their own safety.

In his story of the battle Rain-in-the-Face said:

"I had sung the war-song—I had smelt the powder-smoke—my heart was bad—I was like one who had no mind. I rushed in and took their flag. My pony fell dead as I took it. I jumped up and brained the long-sword flagman with my war-club and ran back to our line with the flag. The long-sword's blood and brains splashed in my face. It felt hot, and blood ran in my mouth. I could taste it. I was mad. I got a fresh pony and rushed back, shooting, cutting, and slashing. This pony was shot, and I got another.

"This time I saw Little Hair [Tom Custer]. I remembered my vow. I was crazy. I feared nothing. I knew nothing would hurt me, for I had my white-weasel-tail charm on. I do not know how many I killed trying to get at him. He knew me. I laughed at him and yelled at him. He was afraid. When I got near enough I shot him with my revolver. I leaped from my pony and cut out his heart and bit a piece out of it and spit it in his face. I got back on my pony and rode off shaking it. I was satisfied and sick of fighting. I didn't scalp him.

"I didn't go back on the field after that. The squaws came up afterward and killed the wounded, cut their boot-legs for moccasin soles, and took their money and watches and rings. They cut their fingers off to get them quicker. They hunted for Long Yellow Hair to scalp him, but could not find him. He didn't wear his fort clothes [uniform], his hair had been cut off, and the Indians didn't know him.

"That night we had a big feast and the scalp dance. Then Sitting Bull came again and made another speech. He said, 'I told you how it would be. I made great medicine. My medicine warmed your hearts and made you brave.'

"He talked a long time. All the Indians gave him the credit of winning the fight because his medicine won it. But, *he wasn't in the fight!* Gall got mad at Sitting Bull that night. Gall said, 'We did the fighting; you only made medicine.' It would have been the same, anyway. Their hearts were bad toward each other after that always. After that fight we could have killed all the others on the hill [Reno's men] but for the quarrel between Gall and Sitting Bull. Both wanted to be head chief. Some of the Indians said Gall was right and went with him, and some said Sitting Bull was."

When news of the Custer catastrophe was received at Fort Leavenworth, Kansas, General Miles and the Fifth Infantry were ordered to go immediately to the scene of the hostilities, and on an autumn day when Lieutenant Otis and his men were escorting a train of supplies from Glendive, Montana, to the cantonment they were attacked by such a fierce body of Indians that the soldiers had hard work to keep their horses from being stampeded and the train from being captured. They finally beat back the Indians, and while there was a momentary cessation of hostilities a messenger rode out from the Indian ranks waving a paper, which he pointedly dropped on a hill in sight. It was picked up and handed to Colonel Otis, who read it.

YELLOWSTONE.

I want to know what you are doing traveling on this road. You scare all the buffalo away. I want to hunt in this place. I want you to turn back from here. If you don't, I will fight you again. I want you to leave what you have got here and turn back from here. I am your friend,

SITTING BULL.

I mean all the rations you have got, and some powder. Wish you would write as soon as you can.

Having read this remarkable document, doubtless written by some half-breed at Sitting Bull's dictation, the colonel sent a scout to Sitting Bull to say that he intended to take his wagon-train through to headquarters in spite of all the Indians alive, and if Sitting Bull wished a fight he would be glad to accommodate him. The train started again, and the Indians promptly resumed their attack, but the combat soon ended in a truce, as the Indians said they were tired and hungry and wanted to treat for peace.

On hearing this, General Otis invited Sitting Bull to come into his line to talk over making such a treaty, but that Sitting Bull refused to do. Two days later, however, General Otis and General Miles overtook the great leader, who then himself asked for an interview, which the general granted for the next day. Sitting Bull was attended by a sub-chief and six warriors, and Miles by an aide and six troopers, when the conference took place. The Sioux chief demanded peace on the old basis. He required for the Indians permission to retain their arms, with liberty to hunt and roam at will over the plains and prairies, with no responsibility to any one. Miles, representing the government, required them to surrender their arms and come into the agencies. Seeing that the conference had been useless, Sitting Bull, standing with his head thrown back, his great chest bared, his eyes bloodshot and gleaming with hatred, declared: "No Indian that ever lived loved the white man, and no white man that ever lived loved the Indian. God Almighty made me an Indian, but not an agency Indian, and I do not intend to be one!"

As his burning words of invective against the white race dropped like red-hot coals from his lips, a young warrior crept to his side and slipped a revolver under his blanket, followed by a dozen other Indians, all evidently meditating treachery, but Miles and his men promptly showed their firearms and ordered them to leave at once. So peremptory was the command that it was obeyed, and a second conference appointed for the next day.

Again Sitting Bull made arbitrary demands. He wished the abandonment by white men of all military posts, and the withdrawal of all settlers from the country which he claimed for his race. Miles, enraged, said that he would no longer treat with a leader who demanded peace at his own terms and would concede nothing to the white men; that he would give him just fifteen minutes to go back to his men and get ready for fighting.

Yelling defiance, chiefs and leader rode back to the Indian lines and made hurried preparations for the fight. Miles, watch in hand, at the appointed moment ordered an advance, and there was a wild battle, lasting until the next day. The intrepid braves again and again rallied their forces to attack the enemy's force, but each time failed, and at last the Indians were driven headlong for forty miles, with a serious loss in warriors, winter supplies, and camp equipage, and three days later two thousand of them surrendered, under promise of good treatment at the agencies. Sitting Bull, however, who had watched the battle at a distance, as usual, prophesying and encouraging his followers, but taking no active part in the combat himself, with Gall and several hundred others refused to give in, and, gathering his forces together, fled to the Canadian line and crossed it. There he and his band were safe for the moment, and were soon joined by the forces of Rain-in-the-Face and Iron Horn.

Although Sitting Bull had not raised a war-club or shot an arrow in defense of his followers' rights, yet still his power remained undiminished, and discontented Indians from the agencies kept on crossing the boundary to join the famous chief's band, because of the government violation of treaty rights and the starvation to which agency Indians were being subjected.

Knowing the large number of Sitting Bull's followers on Canadian soil, commissioners were sent from the United States to try once more to make a treaty of peace with the hostiles, then at Fort Walsh. Being received by the great leader, the white men carefully told of the great kindness of the United States to those who had surrendered, adding, "The President invites you to come to the boundary of his and your country, and there give up your horses, excepting those which are required for peace purposes. Your arms and horses will then be sold, and with all the money obtained for them cows will be bought and sent to you."

As Sitting Bull knew only too well the real treatment given to agency Indians, his reply is not to be wondered at, and is one of the most remarkable protests of an Indian chief against the oppression of his race on record. With calm defiance he faced the commissioners. "For sixty-four years," he said, "you have kept me and my people, and treated us bad. . . . We have done nothing. It is all the people on your side that have started us to do all those depredations. We could not go anywhere else, and we took refuge in this country. . . . The part of the country you gave me you ran me out of. . . . I wish you to go back, and take it easy going!"

He and his followers positively refused to give up their weapons or to exchange their horses for cows, which they did not believe would be given them, for, as Sitting Bull grimly remarked, he had lost faith in a government which had made fifty-two treaties with the Sioux and kept none of them.

Also it did not seem to his men a priceless privilege to be shut up on reservations which they could never leave without being pursued, arrested, and brought back by troops; and the conference closed without any satisfactory results for the government which had sent out the commissioners.

As a parting shot to them Sitting Bull remarked, "Tell them at Washington if they have one man who speaks the truth, to send him to me, and I will listen to what he has got to say!"

Besides the commissioners, several newspaper men were also sent to talk with the great medicine-man who was supposed to have brought about the Custer massacre. Sitting Bull stood to receive his guests, wearing a black-and-white calico shirt, black cloth moccasins and leggings showily embroidered with beads and porcupine quills, and a many-hued blanket hanging from his shoulders. As usual, his head was thrown back in an imperious way, his right foot was forward, and his right arm was folded across his chest, in the manner of an orator. Grasping his visitor's hand, "How!" he exclaimed, "How!" then with a graceful gesture signified where the strangers should sit.

During the conference two Sioux chiefs stood on guard at the door, and all the Indians at the fort were armed and ready to jump in case of unexpected treason, of which they lived in constant dread, but their leader was calm as he listened to the white men's questions.

"You are a great chief, but you live behind a cloud," they said. "Your face is dark; my people do not see it. Tell me, do you hate the Americans very much?"

Sitting Bull's eyes gleamed like black diamonds as he answered:

"I am no chief."

"What are you?"

"I am," he replied, crossing his arms over his chest, with a grim, sardonic smile, "A MAN."

Major Walsh, who was present, hastily explained that he meant, if possible, to keep the strangers in ignorance of his real position among the tribes, adding, "He has constituted himself a ruler, and is a unique power among the Indians, who accept his word as law. He does not assert himself too strongly or interfere with the rights or duties of others; he simply guides his people by his judgment, which has so often been successful that even now his word is worth more than the united voices of the rest of the camp. He speaks, they listen and obey."

The stranger turned to Sitting Bull again. "What is your feeling toward the Americans now?" he asked.

Sitting Bull did not even deign to answer, but touched his hip where his knife hung. The white man persisted.

"Would you live with the Americans in peace if they allowed you to do so, or do you think you can only obtain peace here? The White Mother [Queen Victoria] is good."

"Better than the Great Father? Hough!" A pause, then Sitting Bull said, "They [the commissioners] asked me to give them my horses. I bought my horses, and they are mine. I bought them from men who came up the Missouri. They do not belong to the government, neither do the rifles. The rifles are also mine. I bought them. I paid for them. Why I should give them up I do not know. I will not give them up."

Later he continued, with an air of supreme indifference to his listeners: "I am a man. I see. I know. I began to see when I was not yet born. It was then I began to study about my people. I studied about many things. I studied about the smallpox that was killing my people. I was so interested that I turned over on my side. The

Great Spirit must have told me at that time that I would be the man to be judge of all the other Indians—a big man to decide for them in all their ways."

"And you have since decided for them?"

"I speak. It is enough."

"Could not your people whom you love so well get on with the Americans?"

"No!"

"Why?"

"I never taught my people to trust Americans. I have told them the truth—that the Americans are great liars. I never dealt with the Americans. Why should I? The land belonged to my people. I say I never dealt with them—I mean I never treated with them in a way to surrender my people's rights. I traded with them, but I always gave full value for what I got. . . . I told every trader who came into our camps that I did not want any favors from him, that I wanted to trade with him fairly, giving full value for what I got, but the traders wanted no such terms. They wanted to give little and get much. They told me if I did not accept what they gave me in trade they would get the government to fight me. I told them I did not want to fight."

"But you fought?"

"At last, yes; but not until I had tried hard to prevent a fight. At first my young men, when they began to talk bad, stole five American horses. I was afraid something bad would come of this, so I took the horses away from them and gave them back to the Americans. It did no good. By and by we had to fight."

Still determined to bring about the surrender of the hostiles, in the autumn of 1880 the government sent an army scout, A. H. Allison, together with a soldier in plain clothes, to attempt what had so many times been unsuccessful, and the two men set out with a wagon-load of provisions and presents for the Indians, whom they trailed and finally found in northern Montana, having been driven across the American boundary again in their desperate struggle with starvation.

Sitting Bull at once invited them to stay in his own lodge with his family as long as they cared to remain—doubtless thinking them safer while under his close observation. They accepted the invitation, but Allison at once sought and found Chief Gall, who in a private interview told him that he had determined to make the whole band surrender, but that it would take time. He promised, however, to have at least twenty families ready to accompany Allison when he should leave camp, but cautioned the scout to hide this from Sitting Bull, who was as hostile to the government as ever, and to lead him to believe that the families were only preparing to visit some neighboring tribes.

That night there was a great confusion in camp; the Blackfeet made a raid on the hostiles, and there were hours of heavy fighting, in which Allison and his comrade helped the Sioux defend their property and lives, and by doing this protected their own lives as well. When dawn came all in the camp were in a heavy sleep, and Gall stole to Sitting Bull's lodge, awakened Allison, and they held a whispered conference. Gall told the scout that the twenty families were already on their way down the Milk River, having escaped during the confusion of the raid, that they would encamp and wait for him twenty miles away. Filled with joy at the news, Allison lost no time in leaving camp and journeying down the river, where, as Gall had said, he found the fugitives awaiting his arrival. After refreshing them with a hearty supper, which included good venison, he and his party started on toward Fort Buford, where the twenty families at once surrendered to the government.

Almost as soon as Allison had left, Sitting Bull discovered the escape of the deserters, and that they had been aided in their flight by Chief Gall, who was at once called to a public place to give an explanation of his treachery.

Into the middle of a crowd of muttering savages leaped the intrepid Gall, with characteristic courage, and with never a word of explanation or apology called on all who acknowledged him as chief to separate themselves from Sitting Bull's band and follow him to Fort Buford.

It was the first challenge of Sitting Bull's supremacy. Not for a moment did he dream it would be accepted. What was his horror and amazement to see nearly two-thirds of his braves at once declare allegiance to a new leader! Starvation and hostility had been given a fair chance—now for a change of régime and at least new hopes.

The deserted leader, Sitting Bull, and his remaining followers spent that night and the following ones bound together by their common misery, and as usual at a crisis the mighty medicine-man withdrew to commune with the Great Spirit, who this time seemed to have no inspiring command to give, and on the 20th of July a weary band, headed by their chief, voluntarily surrendered at Fort Buford.

Two days later all the captive hostiles, about two thousand in number, were turned over to the agent at the Standing Rock Agency, North Dakota, where, although Sitting Bull was still hostile to all government demands and decrees, through the following years he was unable to bring about any outbreak of rebellion.

Then some of the Sioux at the agency heard of an Indian, Johnson Sides by name, who was proclaiming the second coming of Christ as the Indian millennium, and by his frenzied descriptions of coming joy arousing intense excitement among many tribes. Several agency Indians even visited him and were thrilled by his glittering promises. Sitting Bull caught the infection, and a gleam of hope flashed through his mind.

He had always been prophet and seer of his people. Here was a chance to mount to a new height of influence and power! He would become a religious teacher, would lead his people in this new frenzy. Clearly his quick mind saw how best to accomplish his end. Withdrawing, as of old, from his tribe for some days, he then reappeared and told in awed, impassioned words of a vision, a meeting with the Messiah, who had told him that his second coming was to rescue the oppressed Indian. Against a background of dramatic imagery, and in a melodious, entreating voice, he spoke of his wonderful revelation, and in a moment was again priest and prophet of his tribe.

The Indians, young and old, swarmed around him, pitching their tepees near his; at his suggestion inaugurated "worship dances," and three thousand frenzied men, women, and children, forming a ring, danced around their leader and his chiefs for hours at a time, chanting weird strains to the music of drum and rattle until they dropped from sheer exhaustion.

The enthusiasm ran like wild-fire through the tribe and agency, as the prophet of the future foretold "the return of their dead ancestors, the restoration of their old Indian life, and the removal of the white race, prophesying that the white man's gunpowder should not in future throw a bullet with sufficient force to injure true believers," adding a long catalogue of such inflaming promises that his converts gave up all practical occupations, left their homes, and spent their time in dancing the ghost dance and in purification baths, both of which occupations were such a hinderance to the usefulness of those who indulged in them that the government tried to put a stop to the craze by arresting Sitting Bull. But he was too clever for them. Up to that time he had gone regularly to the agency to procure his rations, but he now sent a member of his family, and the officers were not able to lay hands on him.

But something must be done to suppress the frenzy, so said the government, and the sooner Sitting Bull could be removed from among the agency Indians, the fewer hostiles there would be to encounter when the outbreak by force came.

A peremptory message from headquarters was sent to the commanding officers at the agency, and everything was put into shape for a quick movement against Sitting Bull, while the major in command quietly sent a company of Indian police in small parties to points on the Grand River above and below the seer's home. They were scattered for some miles, ostensibly cutting timber, but really keeping a close watch on the old leader and his followers.

Then came further orders to secure him immediately, and troops were at once moved forward to reinforce the movements of the Indian police. At dawn on the following morning, while Sitting Bull was sleeping, the police forced an entrance to his lodge and captured him.

Though half dazed by the unexpected arrest, Sitting Bull with majestic calm surrendered, and was preparing to go with the police when his son, Crowfoot, ran to him and began to scold him for yielding so peacefully. Immediately Sitting Bull straightened up, threw back his head in the old way, and, becoming obstinate, refused to go. The police insisted and dragged him forcibly from the house, where they were at once surrounded by a throng of ghost dancers, who were frenzied with rage at having their ceremonies interrupted and by the capture of a leader they had thought more than human.

The policemen shouted commands to the thronging dancers, and finally a space was cleared around Sitting Bull, who was shivering with fear and begging some one to rescue him from the Indian police. He cried out that if the two principal men, Bull Head and Shave Head, were killed, the others would flee. Finally, in as stern a voice as he could command, he shouted to his followers to attack the police.

At once Catch-the-Bear and Strike-the-Kettle dashed through the crowd and fired at the Indians who were guarding Sitting Bull. "Catch-the-Bear's shot struck Bull Head in the side, and he, wheeling, turned on Sitting Bull and shot him in the left side, between the tenth and eleventh ribs; and as Strike-the-Kettle's shot had passed through Shave Head's abdomen, all three fell together. Catch-the-Bear, who fired the first shot, was immediately shot down by Private Lone Man, and the fight became general."

The police at last gained possession of Sitting Bull's lodge and property, and after hours of hard fighting drove the ghost dancers back into the near-by forest, and the Messiah craze, by the loss of its great leader, had received a blow from which it never recovered.

Sitting Bull, the mighty Sioux Medicine-Man, Seer, and Leader, slain by one of his own race, had gone to the happy hunting-grounds to chase the White Buffalo, for ever to be protected by the Great Spirit, who would henceforth guard him from molestations or injustice at the hands of his implacable enemy, the white man.

PONTIAC

PONTIAC: CONSPIRATOR OF THE OTTAWAS

IT was early morning of the 27th of April, 1763, and half a dozen old warriors, heralds of that Indian encampment lately assembled on the banks of the little river Ecorces, not far from Detroit, stalked among the lodges of the assembled men, women, and children, calling out in deep, guttural tones to the warriors to attend the council for which Pontiac, the mighty ruler of the confederacy of Ottawas, Ojibwas, and Pottawottomies, had called together his subjects.

At once the call was answered. "From every wigwam came tall, bronzed figures: Ojibwas with quivers slung at their backs and light war-clubs in their hands; Ottawas wrapped close in gaudy blankets; Wyandots in painted shirts, their heads adorned with feathers and their leggings trimmed with tinkling bells.

"Silently they came together—solemnly they seated themselves in a wide circle on the grass, and so immovable were their savage faces that none could have guessed the depth of ferocious passion and hatred hidden beneath the bronzed masks" as pipes were lighted and passed from hand to hand.

Then Pontiac rose and stood before the listening throng, who thrilled at the sound of his impassioned voice and the sight of his fierce gestures. Superb in vigor and in muscular development he stood before them, bold, stern, and imperious, plumed and painted in the full costume of war, with the bearing of a leader who sweeps aside all opposition by the force of his will.

With a glance over his wild audience, Pontiac spoke:

"It is important, my brothers," he said, "that we should exterminate from our land this nation [the English], whose only object is our death. You must all be sensible that we can no longer supply our wants in the way we were accustomed to do with our fathers, the French. They sell us their goods at double the price that the French made us pay, and yet their merchandise is good for nothing; for no sooner have we bought a blanket or other thing to cover us than it is necessary to procure others against the time of our departure for our wintering-ground. Neither will they let us have them on credit, as our brothers the French used to do. When I visit the English chief and inform him of the death of any of my comrades, instead of lamenting, as our brothers the French used to do, they make game of us. If I ask him for anything for our sick, he refuses and tells us he does not want us, from which it is apparent he seeks our death.

"We must, therefore, destroy them without delay; there are but few of them, and we shall easily overcome them—why should we not attack them? Are we not men? Have I not shown you the belts I received from our Great Father, the King of France? He tells us to strike—why should we not listen to his words? What do you fear? The time has arrived. . . . I have sent belts and speeches to our friends, the Chippewas of Saginaw, and our brothers the Ottawas of Michillimackinac, and to those of the Rivière à la Trauche [Thames River], inviting them to join us, and they will not delay. In the mean time let us strike. There is no longer any time to lose, and when the English shall be defeated we will stop the way so that no more shall return upon our lands."

This and much more said Pontiac, assuring his audience that Indians and Frenchmen would again fight hand in hand as they had in former years.

Lashed into a frenzy of agreement by his fiery words, the Indians grunted assent; and, seeing his words had accomplished their purpose, Pontiac spoke again, this time with quiet eloquence:

"A Delaware Indian," so he said, "conceived an eager desire to learn wisdom from the Master of Life, but, being ignorant where to find him, he had recourse to fasting, dreaming, and magical incantations by which means it was revealed to him how he would reach the abode of the Great Spirit. He told his purpose to none, and, having provided the equipments of a hunter, he set out on his errand, journeying forth in high hope and confidence. After many days of travel, full of strange incidents," continued Pontiac, "he saw before him a mountain so steep that he was about to turn back, when a beautiful woman arrayed in white appeared and said: 'How can you hope, encumbered as you are, to succeed in your design? Go down to the foot of the mountain, throw away your gun, your ammunition, your provisions, and your clothing; wash yourself in the stream which flows there, and you will then be prepared to stand before the Master of Life.'

"The Indian obeyed, and again began to climb among the rocks, while the woman, seeing his discouragement, laughed at him and told him if he would have success he must climb by the aid of one hand and one foot only. He did so, and after great labor and suffering reached the summit of the mountain.

"A rich and beautiful plain lay before him, and in the

distance he saw three great villages, far finer than those of any tribe he had ever visited. He approached the largest, and as he entered a man gorgeously arrayed stepped out and, taking him by the hand, welcomed him to the celestial city, and then led him into the presence of the Great Spirit, where the Indian stood dazzled by the great splendor about him.

"The Great Spirit bade him be seated, and spoke thus to him:

"'I am the Maker of Heaven and Earth, the trees, lakes, rivers, and all things else. I am the Maker of mankind, and because I love you, you must do my will. The land on which you live I have made for you, and not for others. Why do you suffer the white man to dwell among you? My children, you have forgotten the customs and traditions of your forefathers. Why do you not clothe yourselves in skins, as they did, and use the bows and arrows and the stone-pointed lances which they used? You have bought guns, knives, kettles, and blankets from the white men until you can no longer do without them, and, what is worse, you have drunk the poison fire-water, which turns you into fools.

"'Fling all these things away; live as your wise forefathers lived before you. And as for the English—these dogs dressed in red, who have come to rob you of your hunting-grounds and drive away the game—you must lift the hatchet against them. Wipe them from the face of the earth, and then you will win my favor back again and once more be happy and prosperous. The children of your great father, the King of France, are not like the English. Never forget that they are your brethren. They are very dear to me, for they love the red men and understand the true way of worshiping me.'

"Many more precepts for use in daily life did the Great Spirit give the Delaware prophet, after which he was presented with a prayer, embodying all he had heard, cut in Indian characters on a stick, and he was instructed to send copies of the prayer to all Indian villages. He then took his leave, and returned to earth to give a graphic description of the wonders he had seen in his heavenly visit."

Pontiac had used the right method of inflaming his followers, who gladly welcomed the suggestion of a return to their former state of barbarism and were eager to attack the British at once.

Then Pontiac unfolded his great plan—a plan which combined the strategy of the savage with the diplomacy and intelligence of the white man.

"On the second day of May," he said, "there will be a simultaneous attack made on all forts in the possession of the English, each tribe to attack the settlement or fort nearest their encampment. I, myself, will personally conduct the siege of Detroit, because that is the largest and best fortified place to be attacked—thus shall be carried out the command of the Great Spirit in wiping the English off the face of the earth."

There were yells of approval as he finished, and braves, old and young, showed unrestrained joy over the project. The various tribes then made hasty preparations to break camp, and when the sun rose, the village of wigwams on the river Ecorces had melted away, leaving only slight traces of its existence in the silent forest.

Pontiac had called the council because of a momentous crisis in Indian history. Canada and all her dependencies had surrendered to the English, the terms of surrender having been carried out under the command of Major Rogers. All the vast wilderness beyond the Alleghanies over which France had claimed sovereignty had passed into the hands of the British, who believed that the few and inadequately equipped forts guarding their new territory were equal to any emergency which might arise. The hands of the French were now practically tied; the English felt no fear of a serious outbreak among the Indians, so Pontiac's conspiracy was able to ripen into full maturity without even a suspicion of its growth among those against whom the savages were plotting.

During the rule of the French in Canada they had conciliated the Indians in every way, recognizing the value of their good will. Presents had been given them frequently, and at the remote forts surrounding tribes had been supplied with guns, ammunition, food, and clothing until they had come to depend on the white men for their entire support. But an alliance with savage tribes seemed to victorious England of no importance, and she withdrew both gifts and supplies, causing great want as well as many deaths among those Indians from whom the benefits were withheld. "The English fur-traders, too, were in sharp contrast to the French, and cheated and robbed the savages, while the officers and soldiers of those garrisons where of old the Indians had been welcome visitors now met them with blows and orders to 'Be gone!' sometimes emphasized by the touch of a sentinel's musket, a mark of contempt which was unspeakably galling to the proud Indian spirit. But worse than this as a cause for growing discontent among the savages was the invasion of settlers, which was especially felt by those tribes whose lands bordered on the English colonies and who felt an ever-growing resentment at the encroachments of the white men.

All this the French saw, and, believing that through an Indian uprising they might be able in some measure to wreak vengeance on their conquerors, in every way they excited the Indians to concerted action against the British.

Truly the mighty Pontiac had well chosen his time for inflaming the tribes to take part in his great conspiracy!

His plan laid out, Pontiac's opening move was to send to many tribes, among them the Ojibwas of Mackinaw, an invitation to aid him in the war. His messengers, bearing the war-belt of black-and-purple wampum, flung a hatchet painted red at the feet of the assembled warriors of Mackinaw, with a speech which aroused the listeners to such a pitch of frenzy that they took up the blood-red hatchet and pledged themselves to join Pontiac's war.

This decision was quickly followed by the news that the first blow had been struck, which inflamed the Ojibwas to instant action.

At that time there were in the Mackinaw garrison about thirty men and officers under command of Captain Etherington, who had been warned against a possible Indian uprising, but had persistently refused to heed the warning, and on the birthday of the English king had relaxed discipline to such an extent that even the soldiers were allowed special license in honor of the day.

In the near-by woods there was a large encampment of Ojibwas with several bands of Sacs, and early in the morning some Ojibwas went to the fort to invite officers and soldiers to a great game of *baggataway*, or ball, which was to be played between the warriors and the Sacs.

At once the place was deserted by more than half its inhabitants. The gates of the fort stood wide open, Parkman says, unarmed soldiers were collected in groups under the shadow of the palisades, and among them were a great number of Canadians, as well as many Indian squaws wrapped in blankets.

Captain Etherington and Lieutenant Leslie stood near the gate placing bets on the game, as the captain had promised the Ojibwas that he would wager on their side against the Sacs. Indian chiefs and warriors were also among the spectators, apparently intent on the game, but really with thoughts otherwise occupied.

"On went the game. Hundreds of slender, agile figures were running over the plain, each nearly naked, with his loose black hair flying in the wind, and all carrying bats peculiar to the game. At one moment the players were crowded together, all struggling for the ball, at the next they were scattered again, running over the ground, yelling and shouting at the top of their voices. Suddenly the ball was thrown high in the air and fell near the pickets of the fort. Instantly the players ran toward the ball in a whirling, yelling, maddened crowd, but just as they reached the gates the shouts of sport changed into a ferocious war-whoop!

"Squaws threw back their blankets, showing guns, hatchets, and knives, which the players instantly seized instead of their bats, and before the bewildered English had time to think or act the Indians had fallen on the defenseless garrison, butchered fifteen men, captured the others, including the commander, and carried off and destroyed everything belonging to the English."

So much for one incident in Pontiac's conspiracy. During the fifteen days after the massacre at Mackinaw the great chief's followers took possession of Le Bœuf, Venango, Presque Isle, on or near Lake Erie; La Bay, on Lake Michigan; St. Josephs, on the river of that name; Miamis, on the Miami; Ouachtanon, and Sandusky, or every garrison in the West except three. Now Pontiac's most powerful energies were directed toward the taking of Detroit, a settlement

PONTIAC'S ATTACK ON DETROIT

of about twenty-five thousand people, including fur-traders, the ordinary Canadian population, and a well-built fort garrisoned by about three hundred men, under the command of Major Gladwyn.

Despite current rumors of an Indian uprising, when Pontiac arrived there with his warriors they were so intermixed with women and children, and brought so many commodities for trade, that the major had no suspicion of their purpose. The great chief and his band encamped at a little distance from the fort, and at once sent a message to the major that he had come to trade, and wished to talk with him for the purpose of "brightening up the chain of peace" between the English and his people.

To this the unsuspicious major readily agreed, and set the next morning for the interview, giving no further thought to the matter until late that evening, when an Indian woman brought him a pair of elkskin moccasins which he had ordered.

Paying her for the work, the major dismissed her, but she hung around the gates of the fort as they were being closed for the night, refusing to say what she wanted until the major summoned her and demanded her errand. With great hesitation she finally confessed that her real errand was to tell him of an Indian plot against him. The chiefs who were to meet him in council the next day, she said, had planned to murder him and all the other inhabitants and take the garrison. Each chief, she added, would have a gun hidden under his blanket, and while Pontiac was delivering his speech he was to give a signal, at which as many warriors as possible should immediately gather within the fort, all armed, under pretense of trading with the soldiers.

Major Gladwyn heard this with a mixture of astonishment

and incredulity, but, gathering his men together, at once made every preparation to guard the fort against a sudden attack—half of the soldiers were ordered under arms and all of the officers spent the night on the ramparts.

Parkman says: "Again and again Gladwyn mounted his wooden ramparts and looked forth into the gloom. There seemed nothing but repose and peace in the soft air of the warm spring evening. . . . But at intervals as the night wind swept across the bastion it bore sounds of fearful portent, . . . the sullen booming of the Indian drum and the wild chorus of quavering yells, as the warriors around their distant camp-fires danced the war-dance in preparation for the morrow's work; and could the soldiers but have stolen into the forest depths and seen that which was being enacted among the savage tribes there gathered together, their terror would have been doubly great."

The war-chief, "his body painted black from head to foot, after a lonely vigil of fasting and prayer in the deep forest recesses, suddenly emerged from the woods and stood before his followers, who flocked around him as he delivered a wild harangue, calling on them to avenge the blood of their slaughtered relatives, to wipe the hated British off the earth. He assured them that the Great Spirit was on their side—that victory was certain. With exulting cries they dispersed to their wigwams to don the savage decorations of the war-dress. An old man now passed through the camp and invited the warriors to a feast, in the name of the chief, and they gathered from all sides to his wigwam, where they found him seated, no longer covered with black paint, but adorned with the fantastic and startling garb of war-paint. Those who had joined in the feast pledged themselves to follow him against the enemy, then, seating themselves on the ground in a circle around the wigwam, feasted on the flesh of dogs, while the chief, though goaded by the pangs of hunger after his long fast, sat smoking his pipe and taking no part in the repast.

"Night had now closed in, and the clearing was illumined by the blaze of fires and burning pine-knots, casting their deep red glare on the boughs of the surrounding forest, and on the wild multitude who, fluttering with feathers and bedaubed with paint, were ready for the war-dance.

"A painted post was driven into the ground, and the crowd formed a wide circle round it. The chief leaped into the vacant space, brandishing his hatchet as if rushing upon an enemy, and in loud voice related or chanted his own exploits and those of his ancestors, yelling the war-whoop, throwing himself into all the gestures of actual life, striking the post as if it were an enemy, and tearing the scalp from the head of an imaginary victim. Warrior after warrior followed his example until the whole assembly, as if fired with sudden frenzy, rushed together into the ring, leaping, stamping, and whooping, brandishing knives and hatchets in the firelight, hacking and stabbing the air, and breaking at intervals into a burst of ferocious yells which resounded with hideous portent" in the ears of the listening soldiers on the bastion of the fort.

Promptly at the appointed hour on the following morning Pontiac, with thirty-six chiefs and a train of warriors, arrived at the fort, and as the procession of Indians filed into the council-house the Indians exchanged glances of dismay. Every Englishman wore a sword at his side and a pair of pistols in his belt. Boldly Pontiac asked Gladwyn, "Why do I see so many of my father's young men with their guns?"

Gladwyn replied that it was for the sake of exercise and discipline; and, partially satisfied by the explanation, the Indians seated themselves on the skins laid for them, while

Pontiac began his speech, but as he came to the place where he was to give a signal, to his great surprise he noticed Gladwyn and his men all quietly draw their swords half out of their scabbards and the soldiers clutch their guns firmly. The plot had been discovered! But Pontiac was equal to the emergency, and, calmly omitting the expected signal, closed his speech with protestations of respect and affection for the English.

Gladwyn immediately jumped to his feet and charged Pontiac with treachery, told him he knew the whole diabolical plot — that he was powerless to ensnare the English.

Pontiac straightened himself up to his full height and, folding his arms, denied the accusation, whereupon the major pulled aside the blanket of the chief standing nearest him and showed his gun hidden, just as the woman had said it would be.

Pontiac, entrapped and outwitted, bowed his head with assumed meekness, and, without unfolding his arms, led his men from the fort. He was checkmated but not discouraged, and on the next day, taking three chiefs with him, he went again to the fort, carrying the sacred calumet, or pipe of peace. Solemnly he offered it to Gladwyn, saying: "My father, evil birds have sung lies in your ears. We that stand before you are friends of the English. We love them as our brothers, and to prove our love we have come this day to smoke the pipe of peace." Before leaving he gave the pipe to one of the officers as a further pledge of loyalty, and departed to consult with his chiefs—wily commander that he was—on the best method of wiping the hated English off the face of the earth.

Again on the following morning, accompanied by his chiefs, he demanded admittance at the fort, but this time the gates were barred. He shouted to the sentinel to admit him, but Gladwyn himself answered.

"You may enter," he said, "but your followers must remain outside." Pontiac answered that he wished them to enjoy with him and the officers the fragrance of the pipe of peace, but Gladwyn was firm. "You alone may enter," he said. "I will not have that rabble inside the fort again."

This infuriated Pontiac; and, striding away from the fort, he shouted to his followers, who at once leaped from where they were lying, out of reach of gunshot, and all ran off yelling like demons, to work off their rage against the English by killing and scalping as many as they could find to attack. Pontiac himself turned toward the shore, and, Parkman says, "No man durst approach him, for he was terrible in his rage." Jumping into a canoe, he paddled to the Ottawa settlement and shouted to its inmates to move to the west side of the river, nearer the fort, that they might keep a sharper eye on the movements of the garrison. With eager alacrity warriors and squaws began to carry out his commands, and during the night the whole Ottawa settlement crossed the river, pitched their wigwams at the mouth of Parent's Creek, and at dawn a score of the naked savages, yelling like furies, attacked the fort. Hot blazed their guns, a clamor of wild noise filled the still air, and a hail of bullets rained against the walls of the fort for six hours, when the Indians grew weary and went away; and Gladwyn, believing the affair ended, sent La Butte, a neutral interpreter, with two Canadians to Pontiac to open peace negotiations.

The mighty leader, outwardly calm and suave, received his visitors politely, and after a brief conference with his chiefs requested that Major Campbell, second in command at the fort, come himself to confer about this weighty matter.

The message being carried back to Campbell, he was

advised not to undertake such a dangerous mission, but, despite that, at once set off, taking with him a lieutenant and several other men; and when they came near the Indian encampment they were met by a howling mob of women and children armed with clubs, sticks, and stones. Instantly Pontiac strode forward, gorgeous in head-dress and war-paint, and with an imperious gesture quelled the riot, shook hands with the officers, and led the way into camp. Pausing at the entrance to a large lodge, he pointed to mats on the ground. The officers seated themselves, and instantly the council-room was filled with a throng of savages who either stood peering at the British or crouched at the sides of the inclosure. Pontiac spoke a few words to them, which were followed by a long pause. Campbell then made a speech, which was received in silence, and for a whole hour afterward the nerve-racked officers sat with the throng of dark, inscrutable savage faces bending an unwavering gaze on them. At last Campbell could no longer bear it, and, rising, he declared his intention of returning to the fort. With haughty imperiousness Pontiac waved him back to his seat. "My father," he said, "will sleep to-night in the lodges of his red children."

The British officers were in the hands of their enemies!

Many of the Indians were anxious to kill them on the spot; but Pontiac forbade this, and they were taken to the great chief's headquarters and comfortably housed and cared for. One of them afterward escaped; the other, gallant Major Campbell, was tomahawked, and, an old account says, "they boiled his heart and ate it, and made a pouch of the skin of his arms," which brutal deed was unsanctioned by Pontiac.

On the morning after the arrest of the officers Pontiac crossed the river to beg some of the Wyandots, who had refused to take part in the war, to join his forces; and, as he threatened them with destruction if they remained neutral any longer, they reluctantly gave in and declared themselves his allies. He then resumed operations with new vigor and placed his forces to better advantage, one band lying in ambush along the river, below the fort, while others surrounded it on the land side, and, so placed, made no further attack on the fort until the 11th of May, when six hundred of them began a brisk firing which was kept up until seven in the evening, when a Canadian carried a summons to Gladwyn from Pontiac demanding his surrender. To this Gladwyn gave a flat refusal, and the Indians continued their attacks day after day, until their war-cries and the rattle of their guns became familiar sounds to the soldiers, who for many weeks slept in their clothing and with their weapons by their side.

The savages resorted to every known device and stratagem to rout the English enemy: at one time they filled a cart with combustibles and ran it against the pickets to set them on fire; at another they would have fired the church had not a French priest told Pontiac that this would draw down the anger of God on him, when they desisted. They tried to cut down the pickets so as to make an opening in the wall of the fort, on discovering which Major Gladwyn ordered his soldiers to help them cut, when an opening was quickly made. The Indians made a wild rush for it, but a cannon was instantly fired from the inside, and many Indians were killed.

During the succeeding months the fort was blockaded and its supplies cut off, which reduced the garrison to such distress that, had it not been for provisions secretly carried to them by an old Canadian under cover of darkness, Detroit would have been destroyed or abandoned.

The Indians, too, were suffering for lack of provisions, and, visiting Canadian families along the river, demanded food, threatening violence if it were refused; and when it was given, they wasted it with characteristic carelessness. At last in despair the Canadians sent fifteen men to Pontiac with complaints.

Pontiac sat immovable, his eyes cast on the ground, his arms folded, listening. Then with a haughty toss of the head he addressed the chiefs assembled from neighboring tribes:

"Brothers, we have never wished to do you harm nor allow any to be done you; but among us there are many young men who, though strictly watched, find opportunities for mischief. It is to revenge you, my brothers. When the English insulted us, they insulted you also. . . . I mean to destroy the English and leave not one upon our lands. . . . I know, my brothers, that there are many among you who take part with the English. I am sorry for it, for their own sakes, for when our father arrives I shall point them out to him, and they will see whether they or I have the most reason to be satisfied with the part we have acted."

Turning to the Canadians, he continued: "It is now seventeen years since the Ojibwas, with the Sacs and Foxes, came down to destroy you. Who then defended you? Was it not I and my young men? Mickinac, great chief of all these nations, said in council that he would carry to his village the head of your commandant—that he would eat his heart and drink his blood. Did I not take your part? Did I not go to his camp and say to him that if he wished to kill the French he must first kill me and my warriors? Did I not assist you in routing and driving him away? And now you think that I would turn my arms against you! No, my brothers, I am the same French Pontiac who assisted you seventeen years ago. . . . I am a Frenchman, and I wish to die a Frenchman; and now I repeat to you that I should be avenged. I do not ask you for aid, for it is not in your power to give it. I only ask for provisions for myself and men. Yet if you are inclined to assist me I shall not refuse you. It would please me, and you yourselves would be sooner rid of your troubles, for I promise you that as soon as the English are driven out we will go back to our village and there await the arrival of our French father. You have heard what I say: remain in peace, and I will watch that no harm shall be done to you either by my men or by other Indians."

Pontiac had said his say; at the end of the council he took prompt measures to bring the disorders complained of to an end, and in doing this showed a policy scarcely paralleled in the history of his race. He first forbid any further outrages, under the severest penalty; then he visited the homes of the Canadians, and, after inspecting the property belonging to them, assigned to each the share of provisions they must furnish for the support of the Indians. These contributions were all collected at one place, where they were distributed to the various tribes, under the personal supervision of the great chief; but what stamped him as the born commander—the Indian Napoleon—was a still greater stroke of diplomacy. Anxious not to offend the Canadians, but, unable to pay for the provisions he had levied, he issued promissory notes, drawn on birch-bark and signed with the figure of an otter, the totem of his family. Under this was drawn a picture of the particular article for which the bill was good—as a gun, a bag of corn, a deer, a hog, or a cow. These bills passed current among the Canadians and Indians of the period, and were faithfully redeemed after the war, an example worthy of imitation by Pontiac's modern successors.

Not an Ottawa dared disobey the chief's command, and the Canadians' property was respected from that time. Some young Wyandots, however, still made nightly raids on the hog-pen of an old friend of Pontiac's, who, hearing of this, himself crept out in the darkness and surprised the thieves by shouting: "Go back to your village, you Wyandot dogs. If you tread again on this man's land, you shall die!"

Abashed, the Wyandots slunk away, with no thought of disobeying Pontiac's command, although he could claim no legitimate authority over them.

Weeks went by, and still the Indians kept a keen-eyed watch on the fort, where officers and men were eagerly awaiting the coming of a strong force of regulars, under Major Cuyler, sent for their relief. The boats of this expedition were known to be approaching, but, as day succeeded day without their arrival, anxiety was felt at the fort, and Gladwyn despatched a vessel to Niagara to hasten forward the expected convoy. Then came a sudden lifting of gloom in the garrison, faces again wore expressions of joy and expectancy—the long-looked-for vessels had been sighted!

Parkman says: "With one accord the garrison broke into three hearty cheers, while a cannon sent its loud voice of defiance to the enemy and welcome to the approaching friends. But suddenly every cheek grew pale with horror. Dark, naked figures were seen rising with wild gestures in the boats, while in place of the answering salute the distant yells of the war-whoop fell faintly on their ears. The convoy was in the hands of the enemy—the boats had all been taken and the troops of the detachment under Major Cuyler slain or made captive!"

While the English were still overcome by this terrible loss, Pontiac's forces had been strengthened by the arrival of two fierce bands of Ojibwas, making a whole number of eight hundred and twenty warriors, who, encamping with a great number of squaws and children in the fields and forests near the fort, must have made a picturesque and stirring scene.

For the beleaguered garrison those were days of gloom and incessant attacks, but again came a ray of hope on the 19th of June, when the vessel which Gladwyn had sent to hasten Major Cuyler's convoy came in sight. Though it encountered a fierce attack from the Indians as it entered the narrowest part of the channel, it was able to sail up to the fort at last and anchor quietly, and brought not only men, ammunition, and supplies for the beleaguered garrison, but also the important news that peace had at last been declared between France and England—that henceforth they would be allies.

When this was told Pontiac he refused to believe it, and with new zest called for a council with the Canadians, hoping to gain them for new allies. A motley throng of half-breeds, Canadians, trappers, and Indians wrapped in gay blankets and decorated with paint and feathers gathered at his command, and when they were all seated, and pipes had been passed from hand to hand, Pontiac stood before them and flung a war-belt at the feet of the Canadians.

"My brothers," he exclaimed, "how long will you suffer this bad flesh to remain on your lands? You call yourselves our friends, and yet you assist the English with provisions and go about as spies among our villages. This must not continue. You must either be wholly French or wholly English. If you are French, take up the war-belt and lift the hatchet with us; but if you are English, then we declare war against you. My brothers, I know this is a hard thing. We are all alike children of our great father, the King of France, and it is a hard thing to fight among brethren for the sake of dogs. But there is no choice. Look upon that war-belt, and let us hear your answer."

An old Canadian made quick reply. He professed great love for the Indians and a strong desire to help them in their war, but, drawing out a copy of the capitulation of Montreal and its dependencies, which included Detroit, he showed it as an argument against further alliance with the red men.

Mortified, enraged, and baffled, Pontiac was almost ready to acknowledge defeat, when a number of forest vagabonds took up the war-belt, declaring that they were ready to fight on his side. This so cheered him that he spent the night feasting and dancing in honor of his new allies, and continued hostilities.

But all his moves now met with defeat, and the Wyandots and Pottawottomies began to tire of such an endless task as this siege was proving. Demanding audience of Major Gladwyn, they begged for peace, which the major thankfully granted on the condition that all English prisoners in Indian villages be surrendered. This was agreed to, and only the Ojibwas and Ottawas remained to carry on the siege. From that time little of importance happened at the fort until the end of July, when Captain Dalzell arrived with two hundred and eighty men, several small cannon, ammunition, and supplies.

He arrived at night, and after a conference with Gladwyn was eager to go out at once and attack the Indians. Gladwyn firmly opposed this, but Dalzell had his way, and about two o'clock in the morning the gates of the fort were thrown open in silence and the new detachment passed noiselessly out, filing two deep along the road, while two large boats, each with a swivel on the bow, rowed up the river abreast of the troops, with orders to keep up with the line of march, cover a retreat, and carry off the wounded.

"On the men marched for over a mile, to the mouth of Parent's Creek, since called Bloody Run, where the road crossed the creek by a wooden bridge. Just beyond this the land rose in ridges parallel to the stream, along the summit of which Pontiac had caused intrenchments to be made to protect his former camp. Here were two piles of wood, picket fences, and gardens belonging to neighboring Canadians; and behind every fence and intrenchment and woodpile crouched Indians, silent as snakes, listening to the tramping of the approaching soldiers. On they came, and the advance-guards were half-way across the bridge when there was a horrible chorus of yells in front of them, while the Indians advanced and poured such a hot fire of bullets on them that many fell at once." Dalzell's ringing voice rallied them to renewed efforts, but in vain, and his speedy death demoralized the whole force.

Major Rogers, with twenty rangers and some regulars, took possession of a house by the roadside, and, barricading the windows, held the Indians at bay. Captain Grant hurried forward and took another strong position by the river, ordering the boats to anchor near the house where Rogers and his men were and open fire on the attacking Indians force. While this was being done, Major Rogers and his men were able to make the fort under cover of darkness and the cannonade, having had fifty-nine men killed and wounded, while the Indians escaped with a comparatively small loss—a striking example of Pontiac's ability as a commander.

The Indians were so elated by this victory that runners were sent out for several hundred miles through the woods to spread the tidings, and reinforcements soon began to come in to swell the force of Pontiac; but even so it was not doubted that the English would succeed in defending the fort, and the days passed with only a few skirmishes until the 4th of September.

Then the schooner *Gladwyn* was returning from Niagara, having on board her master, her mate, and a crew of ten men, besides six Iroquois Indians, supposed to be friendly to the English. On the night of September 3rd she sailed into the Detroit River, and in the morning the Indians asked to be set on shore.

The request having been foolishly granted, they disappeared in the woods, and, seeking Pontiac, reported the small crew of the *Gladwyn*. Parkman says: "The vessel stood up the river until nightfall, when, the wind failing, she was compelled to anchor about nine miles below the fort. . . . The night set in with darkness so complete that at the distance of a few rods nothing could be discerned. Meanwhile three hundred and fifty Indians in their birch canoes glided silently down with the current and were close upon the vessel before they were seen.

"There was only time to fire a single cannon-shot among them before they were beneath her bows and clambering up her sides, holding their knives clenched fast between their teeth. The crew gave them a close fire of musketry without any effect; then, flinging down their guns, they seized the spears and hatchets and met the assailants with such furious energy and courage that in a couple of minutes they had killed and wounded more than twice their own number. But the Indians were only checked for a moment. The master of the vessel was killed, several of the crew were disabled, and the Indians were leaping over the bulwarks when the mate called out, 'Blow up the schooner!'

"This desperate command saved her and her crew. Some Wyandots who had gained her deck caught the meaning of his words and gave the alarm to their companions. Instantly every Indian leaped overboard in a panic, and the whole were seen diving and swimming off in all directions to escape the threatened explosion. The schooner was cleared of her assailants, who did not dare to renew the attack, and on the following morning she sailed for the fort, which she reached without molestation. Only six of her crew re-escaped unhurt, and their appearance was enough to convince every one of their bravery, they being as bloody as butchers, and their bayonets, spears, and cutlasses blood up to the hilt."

Cuyler's disastrous expedition and the Bloody Run fatality, added to the fact that nine out of the twelve frontier posts had been captured by Pontiac's forces, now led Sir Jeffrey Amherst, commander-in-chief of the English army, to the conclusion that it was time to use drastic measures to bring about the subjection of the Indians, and he sent two armies into the Indian country—one under Colonel Bouquet to Fort Pitt, the other under Colonel Bradstreet up the lakes to Detroit—which he was commanded to force into unconditional subjection.

Colonel Bouquet, after a two days' battle at Bushy Run, reduced the red men to beg for peace, which news was immediately carried to Pontiac, together with the report that Colonel Bradstreet was coming to Detroit with three thousand men. Only too well the great conspirator knew that now he would not be able to hold out much longer against the hated white men and their iron grasp, as many of his former allies were deserting him and French assistance was becoming a dream.

Long and deeply Pontiac pondered on the situation, and, as a result of his meditation, before Bradstreet had time to reach Detroit the mighty leader and his Ottawas abandoned the siege temporarily and retreated to camp on the Maumee, in the Illinois country.

Pontiac's view of the situation was correct; his power was broken. On his way to Detroit, Bradstreet stopped at Niagara to meet Sir William Johnson and hold a council with two thousand Indians of twenty-two tribes, all of whom now showed a desire to make peace with the English and denied connection with Pontiac's conspiracy. Well satisfied, Bradstreet journeyed on to Detroit. Pontiac had fled, but his remaining allies at once made a treaty of peace, and the siege which had been kept up for over fifteen months was ended. But Pontiac refused to be concerned in the treaty, and sent word that "When he made peace it should be such a one as would be useful and honorable to himself and to the King of Great Britain. But he has not as yet proposed his terms!"

In his camp on the Maumee the great leader now decided on a last desperate struggle against the English. He would rally the western tribes of Illinois and Indiana into a new confederation to resist the English invaders if they attempted to advance into the Illinois country.

Visiting M. Neyon, commandant at the fort, Pontiac laid before him a large belt of wampum. "My father," he said, "I come to invite you and your allies to go to war with me against the English."

In reply Neyon asked him if he had not received his letter of the last autumn, telling him that henceforth the French and English nations were to be as one people. Pontiac apparently did not hear, and again urged Neyon to go to war with him, whereupon Neyon lost patience with him, and, kicking the belt away from his feet, asked angrily if Pontiac were deaf.

With one long, inscrutable glance of scorn, Pontiac turned

away in silence and returned to the Maumee, where he remained until late autumn.

Then once more he started out with his four hundred faithful warriors, all glittering in wonderful head-dresses and brilliant with war decorations. Crossing the Wabash, they went from village to village among the Kickapoos and the three tribes of the Miamis, rousing in them a reflection of Pontiac's own spirit of fierce rebellion and resistance. Then by rapid marches they crossed to the banks of the Mississippi, and Pontiac called together the four tribes of the Illinois in a general council. But these tribes showed no interest either in warfare or in assisting him, and he stood before them quivering with anger, exclaiming, "If you hesitate, I will consume your tribe as a fire consumes the dry grass on the prairie!"

So terrible was he in his anger that the Illinois, as one man, instantly declared their loyalty to his cause, hiding their venom at his words with true Indian concealment; and Pontiac departed content.

He next went to Fort Chartres, where Saint-Ange, commander-in-chief, heard his request for arms, ammunition, and troops with courtesy, but firmly refused to grant the request. This so angered Pontiac that he commanded his warriors to pitch their tents directly outside of the fort, to worry the French with constant symptoms of an attack, while he was having his squaws hurriedly make a belt of wampum six feet long and four inches wide, worked from end to end with the symbols of the various tribes and villages still belonging to his alliance. Then, picking out his finest warriors, he gave them the belt to carry down the Mississippi, and display at every Indian village along the river-banks, urging the tribes in the name of the mighty Pontiac to closely watch the movement of the English and repel any attempt they might make to ascend the river. This done, the ambassadors were to go to New Orleans and demand of its governor the aid which Saint-Ange had refused; but all attempts to rally his forces to victory against the hated enemy failed.

His ambassadors came back from the country east of the Mississippi with the report that France had transferred her remaining American possessions to Spain, and all hope of aid in that quarter was dashed.

To this report was added news of failure all along the line of march; Pontiac's followers were now daily dropping off from their allegiance.

Parkman says: "In the South lay the Cherokees, hereditary enemies of his people; in the West were the Osages and Missouris, treacherous and uncertain friends, and the fierce and jealous Dakotas. In the East the forests would soon be full of English traders and beset with English troops; while in the North his own village of Detroit lay beneath the guns of the victorious garrison.

"Pontiac's mighty plan, the work of a master mind, had failed. The arch-conspirator might have now sought refuge in a still more remote wilderness of the upper lakes, but this would have doomed his aspiring spirit to a life of unambitious exile. In a night of gloomy brooding he determined now to smoke the calumet with his triumphant enemies, though the fire of hatred in his heart was still a blood-red flame.

"His stormy spirit had warred with destiny, and had been conquered." There had remained for him two alternatives: to be destroyed by the hand of the enemy or to submit to their decree. Hot with anger, he had chosen the latter, and started for Fort Quiatenon, on the Wabash, to meet George Croghan, an English commissioner, to whom he must formally tender the traditional pipe of peace.

PONTIAC

In a forest near the fort, Croghan's forces met the long train of warriors headed by the great Pontiac. Fear was visible on every English face, but Pontiac calmly advanced and held out his hand to Croghan, and the two forces marched on together to the fort, where Pontiac not only offered the calumet and belt of peace, but declared friendship for the English.

Then, in Croghan's company, Pontiac and his followers marched on to Detroit, which they reached on the 17th of August. There was, as in the days of Pontiac's siege, a great gathering of Ottawas, Ojibwas, and Pottawottomies around the fort, but now all were as eager to become allies of the English as they had before been anxious to wage war against them—for they saw clearly that there was nothing further to be gained by loyalty to France or to Pontiac.

For ten days the bands of Indians and Croghan's men remained together without any new agreement; then Croghan called a meeting of the assembled tribes and spoke to them, using the figurative language of the Indian. "Children," he said, "we are very glad to see so many of you here present at your ancient council-fire, which has been neglected for some time past; since then high winds have blown and raised heavy clouds over your country. I now, by this belt, rekindle your ancient fire and throw dry wood upon it, that the blaze may ascend to heaven, so that all nations may see it and know that you live in peace and tranquillity with your fathers, the English.

"Children, by this belt I gather up all the bones of your deceased friends and bury them deep in the ground, that the buds and sweet flowers of the earth may grow over them, that we may not see them any more.

"Children, with this belt I take the hatchet out of your hand and pluck up a large tree, and bury it deep, so that it may never be found any more; and I plant the tree of peace, which all our children may sit under and smoke in peace with their fathers.

"Children, we have made a road from the sunrising to the sunsetting. I desire that you will preserve that road good and pleasant to travel upon, that we may all share the blessings of this happy union.

"By this belt I disperse all the black clouds from over your heads, that the sun may shine clear on your women and children, that those unborn may enjoy the blessings of this general peace, now so happily settled between your fathers the English and you, and all your younger brethren, to the sunsetting."

To this speech, with all its suggestive allusions, Pontiac listened with folded arms and inscrutable calm, and doubtless pondered on it in the hours of the night. The next day he made this response at a great gathering of English and Indians.

"Father," he said, "we have all smoked the pipe of peace. It is your children's pipe; and as the war is all over, and the Great Spirit and Giver of Light, who has made the earth and everything therein, has brought us together this day for our mutual good, I declare to all nations that I have settled my peace with you before I came here, and now deliver my pipe to be sent to Sir William Johnson, that he may know I have made peace and taken the King of England for my father, in presence of all the nations now assembled; and whenever any of those nations go to visit him they may smoke out of it with him in peace. Fathers, we are obliged to you for lighting up our old council-fire for us and desiring us to return to it; but we are now settled on the Miami River, not far from hence; whenever you want us, you will find us there."

PONTIAC

In the council-hall, where Pontiac and his warriors had once attempted to destroy the garrison, the terms of peace were now formally arranged and ratified by representatives for the Ojibwas and Pottawottomies; and Pontiac, in accordance with his pledged word, a few months later visited Sir William Johnson at his castle on the Mohawk, and on behalf of all the tribes lately banded together in his confederation concluded a treaty of peace with the English in these words:

"Father, when our great father of France was in this country I held him fast by the hand. Now that he is gone, I take you, my English father, by the hand, in the name of all the nations and promise to keep this covenant as long as I shall live. . . ."

Here he delivered a large belt of wampum, adding:

"Father, when you address me it is the same as if you address all the nations of the West. Father, this belt is to cover and strengthen our chain of friendship, and to show you that if any nation shall lift the hatchet against our English brethren we shall be the first to feel and resent it."

This speech he followed by a promise to recall the war-belts which had been sent to the North and West. Then other chiefs addressed the Western nations, urging them to hold fast the bond of friendship, and the council closed with a lavish distribution of presents to Pontiac and his warriors. Thus ended the memorable meeting in which the great Pontiac sealed his submission to the English and gave up the fulfilment of that conspiracy which had been his cherished ideal.

A mighty leader of his nation was he, this Indian Napoleon: his vices were those of his people; his virtues those of the best minds of the white race; and in his conspiracy there was a breadth of purpose never exceeded among savage tribes.

Though slain by one of his own race in a spirit of fierce revenge for injuries received in earlier days; though baffled in his purpose and unsuccessful in his daring achievement, yet is the name of the great Pontiac one still to conjure with among white leaders and Indian devotees.

THE END